How Arcturians Are Healing Planet Earth

One Soul or Millions at a Time

Wayne Brewer

Printed in the United States of America
ISBN: 978-0-9856133-0-3

Library of Congress Control Number: 2011919379

Published by
Wayne Brewer
11024 Montgomery Blvd. NE, No. 260
Albuquerque NM 87111
www.WayneBrewer.net

Table of Contents

Preface

D ue to the provocative nature of the contents of this book, the names of everyone involved in the healing sessions, except mine, have been changed for their protection and privacy. However, all of the stories related are true, and all the sessions, whether in-person or at-a-distance, were tape-recorded and transcribed to insure accuracy.

You may find that you are having an adverse reaction of some kind—mental, emotional, or physical—right now as you are reading this, or you may find that you have a negative reaction as you try reading the rest of the book. *That reaction may indicate you have entities of one type or another, which is all the more reason for you to continue reading so you can learn more and find out what to do about them.* Always remember that the darkness is no match for the Light. Light always defeats darkness. Don't despair, and don't let any of these entities control you any longer.

Some of the events and experiences you will read about took place only a few months prior to the book's publication. My learning and understanding have continuously evolved over the course of several years. One thing has led to or built upon another, and each new discovery has broadened my understanding even as it has raised more questions. I don't expect this progression to stop upon publication of this book. If you are interested in keeping up with new information as it is revealed to me, you can sign up for my free periodic newsletter by visiting my website, www.WayneBrewer.net.

I want to give special thanks, love, and appreciation to Carl, Robert, and Lisa for their courage in continuing to participate, especially when we had no idea who or what we were dealing with. I also want to acknowledge and express my gratitude to everyone who has been involved in the preparation of this book and everyone who has been on this journey with me and has helped me learn and evolve.

I especially want to give thanks to the Arcturians, who have been the greatest transforming influence in my life. They gave me this message to pass along to all of you:

We lovingly suggest you set your ego aside and read through this document quickly but with an open mind. Then go back and reread it slowly, with an open heart, to reap the fullest benefit both for yourself and for your beloved planet Earth. Listen to your intuition and you will know without a shadow of a doubt the truth that is revealed within these pages.

Introduction

There's a forested place in the Zuni Mountains of New Mexico, out in the middle of nowhere, where I've been going camping for at least 20 years. I take a lot of photographs, but this is the only campsite photo I've ever framed, and for years I've kept it near me on my desk: red rock overlook and scraggly vegetation in the foreground, blue mountains in the distance, and in the middle, a valley under a blue sky filled with puffy clouds.

There isn't really anything special about this particular location; I just like it. It makes me feel good. I used to take my kids there, and now I visit it every once in a while, often by myself. Being in the mountains or the forest recharges me, so I go there to relax for a day, sometimes longer.

On July 18, 2009, I decided to camp up there overnight. I've never encountered any other people in the area—only bears and other animals—so I always take a gun with me. In fact, I've never gone into the wilderness without taking one. But while I was packing for the trip, I was about to get my gun when a telepathic message came through loud and clear: *Don't do it!* I had no idea why I wasn't supposed to take it, but I left the gun behind.

At the campsite that evening, I was sitting in a little chair, trying to finish the book I was reading about how to release discarnate spirits and send them to the Light. It was hot, and there was barely a breeze to disturb the peaceful nature of the place—that is, until a huge Black Angus bull wandered into a meadow down in the valley, bellowing and bellowing, looking for some cows and calves. I was raised on a farm and have been around farm animals all my life. I'd never heard a bull bellow as loudly and insistently as that one did, and I wondered why it was behaving that way.

Before the bull had even shown up, I'd already been feeling a lot of extraordinary energy. I also suddenly felt cold and had to put on a long-sleeved shirt and a jacket even though the temperature was nearly 80 degrees. The sun was setting, but there was still enough light to read by so I went back to my book. When I glanced up briefly, I looked right back down again and said to myself, "I didn't see that."

But what I had seen standing out there in the meadow, staring at me and waiting—they were obviously waiting for me—were maybe a hundred *beings.* They were not in human form, not even in physical form. I could only see them from about mid-thigh up. I couldn't see them touching the ground. It was as though they were manifesting just enough of themselves to make me aware of them.

Somehow I managed to convince myself I had not seen them. I was nearly at the end of the book so I continued reading until the sun went down and I couldn't read anymore. I didn't give the startling vision another thought. Sometime around nine o'clock, I closed the book, looked up, and said, "Oh, my God." These beings had filled the entire meadow as if they were an audience waiting for a rock concert to begin. They just stared at me; nobody even waved a hand.

Then it dawned on me that it was the book I'd been reading that had called them in. *Let's go to the Light. It's time to go to the Light.* And somehow I knew exactly what to do. My guides led me through it. I stood up and declared the area holy ground. Then I created a vortex, which is like a swirling shaft of light, but more powerful, and these beings started going up into the vortex. As I continued to hold the vortex open, I heard the message, "They're coming from 30 miles around." So I called them in. "Anybody else? Anybody else?" After most of them had gone, I happened to look up about 30 feet in the air, and there was another one heading straight for that vortex, floating through the trees in a running position. As soon as he got to the vortex, he went straight up, too. When I asked how many there were, my guides said, "2,000," which seemed about right to me.

When they were all gone, I asked, "Who were they?" The guides only gave me a one-word answer, "ancients." Not "the ancients," but "ancients." I had no idea what they meant, and I still don't. Maybe they were Anasazi ancients—or even ancestors of the Anasazi. I guess that's not something I need to know. But even now I feel some of their appreciation at being able to go to the Light—finally, after all this time.

Later I realized that if I'd taken my gun with me, this probably wouldn't have happened. They wouldn't have shown themselves to me. That wasn't the kind of energy that was needed for this particular mission—a mission I didn't even know I was going out there to accomplish. That was the first time I created a vortex, and I'm not sure who was helping me then. I didn't yet know the Arcturians, but perhaps they were already guiding me.

PART ONE

Chapter 1
Tapped In, Tuned In, Turned On

Leaving My Comfort Zone

I've been in the investigative business for over 35 years. In the course of conducting an investigation, I collect information from as many reliable sources as possible, as well as from my own physical observations. Then I report the facts to the client and let the client draw his or her own conclusions. That's the world I've been at home in, the world of logic and so-called objective reality. So to say I was skeptical about some of the non-rational experiences I began having would be a huge understatement. But one incident finally made it crystal clear to me that I could no longer discount these personal experiences or explain them away logically.

In November 2008, I was working in Houston, Texas after Hurricane Ike had struck Galveston that September. I'd been there about a month, putting in a lot of hours every day with no time off. When I wasn't working, I was reading. I'd begun meditating earlier in the year, and at that time I was reading about the Law of Attraction[1].

One night in my hotel room, I was sitting up in bed with a book when my left arm began quivering. At first, that didn't seem at all unusual. I had been in a skiing accident in 1992 and fractured my left humerus and the ball of my shoulder socket in twelve places. Ever since, my arm twitches or quivers periodically, especially when I'm doing what I call decompressing—trying to relax after a period of working non-stop.

That's only one of the physical injuries I've had, almost all of them on the left side of my body. The summer before starting kindergarten, I was helping out on the family farm moving bales of hay when my left hand got caught in a pulley. The accident nearly took my little finger off, and to this day, the joint won't bend due to the calcification. A few years ago, I ran into an old acquaintance who remembered my hand had been bandaged when I'd started kindergarten. He wanted to look at it, so I showed him the scar across my palm.

As far as the shoulder injury was concerned, I'd been to see all kinds of conventional and alternative medical practitioners about it over the years, including medical doctors, a naturopath, several chiropractors, and various massage therapists. One said one thing; another said something else. But I'd always assumed there was a neurological basis for the twitching.

But then, all of a sudden in that Houston hotel room, my arm flailed back and forth in a wide arc as if it were waving. The force was so strong it actually pulled me across the bed! I had no idea what was happening. The only thing I was certain of was that the cause couldn't possibly be neurological.

Shortly after that, I left Houston and returned home to Albuquerque. I wanted to get back to see my good friend, Carmen, who was experi-

---

[1] You can learn more about the Law of Attraction in the book of the same name by Esther and Jerry Hicks.

encing some medical problems. Carmen had introduced me to the book *The Secret*[2] and had played a significant role in starting me on this journey. Although I didn't know exactly what her medical problems were, somehow I knew I could help her. I wasn't sure *how* or *why* I could help; I just knew I could. I had a very strong feeling that I needed to lay my hands on her back.

When I saw Carmen and placed my hands on her back, the energy that went through me was so intense she thought I was going to have a heart attack. I could barely handle that much energy then. Although at the time I didn't fully understand what had happened, I did know some kind of healing had taken place with her. Of course, I wanted to learn more. I wanted to understand what was going on.

Consulting a Psychic

Even before I went to Houston, my curiosity had been piqued by some of my experiences and the metaphysical books I'd been reading. I'd gone as far as making an appointment with a well-known Albuquerque psychic and channel. I hadn't actually met her, but I'd known of her for years. She holds weekly channeling sessions at the Albuquerque Center for Spiritual Living, and I'd attended two or three times just to observe. During the sessions, she channels her spirit guide, Orion, and then invites people to ask her questions.

I had never participated or even spoken to her. After the sessions, while everyone else was lining up to talk to her or give her a hug, I was heading out another door. But I'd look over at her, and we'd exchange glances and nod at each other. That was the extent of our interaction.

It was after checking out the channeling sessions that I'd made my appointment with her, but I'd had to cancel it to go to Houston. So as soon as I returned home, I scheduled another appointment. My first meeting with her was as confusing and disconcerting as it was revealing. She seemed to assume I knew a lot more than I did at the

[2] *The Secret*, written by Rhonda Byrne, is another book on the Law of Attraction.

time. Right from the beginning, I've been playing catch-up in the metaphysical realm—first having experiences I can't explain and then doing the research to try figure out what they mean.

She let Orion talk to me for about 30 minutes. Orion, a collective consciousness that vibrates at a higher level than we humans do, kept addressing me as "John." "We're so happy to be able to reconnect with you, John." I'm not entirely clear about this, but Orion suggested I may have a connection with John the Baptist. Orion also told me a great deal about my personal history and relationships, including several past lives, and confirmed that my friend Carmen and I have known each other over multiple lifetimes, which explains the close bond we have.

What I really wanted to find out about was what was going on with my arm. Was there some kind of healing energy in it, as I suspected? Orion said yes, but his answer went beyond that. Orion told me I would be performing miracles in three months. *Miracles?* Me? That was just too far-fetched. I couldn't buy it. Orion said that at first I wouldn't believe the things that would happen. I'd be astounded. Well, that part has certainly turned out to be true. I have definitely been astounded—more and more so every day.

Learning to Channel and Meeting My Guides

In spite of my strong skepticism, less than a month later, I started taking the first of a series of three channeling classes. In the first class, C1, you go into a light trance, a channeled state, to find out who your three main guides are, and you learn how to connect with them. You get out of your head, out of your ego, and drop into your heart: *tapped in, tuned in, turned on* is what I call it.

But I already knew who one of my guides was.

During my first meeting with the psychic, when she told me I would be an excellent candidate for channeling, I blurted out, "Who's Raphael?" That name had been coming up in my mind for a long time. There's a little town south of Grants, New Mexico called San Rafael, and every time I've driven past it, I've always noticed how good I feel. San Rafael is also the name of the street that goes up to my house. I had always felt Raphael was with me, but I'd thought he was simply a guardian angel or something like that. It wasn't until the C1 class that I learned he is actually an archangel.

At the time your guides make themselves known to you, each one presents you with a gift. Raphael gave me something I already had, which was a red wooden heart with a candle in it that I'd bought at an Asian art store. I was shopping with Carmen when I first saw it, and she remarked on how much energy it had. I didn't feel the energy at the time, but I liked it, so the next day, I went back and got it. That's the gift Raphael presented to me.

Jesus is another of my guides. I've always known he's been with me, too. He gave me an open Bible, which he pressed into my heart chakra[3]. Then Athena came in, and that really confused me. Who was Athena? The mythical Greek Goddess? I had no idea, but she gave me a color, violet, which is the highest vibrational color the human eye can see.

I took the C1 class solely to connect with my guides. I had no other expectations and no intention of taking any more classes. But a month later, there I was at the C2 class, which is kind of a refresher of what was learned in C1. Then I went on to take C3. I actually found the C3 class kind of embarrassing. For one thing, I was the only guy in it. For another, many of the people in the class had been involved in this kind of *woo-woo* stuff, as I called it, for years and knew a lot more than I did. I was still playing catch-up, listening to what everyone said, taking lots of notes, and then doing my own research.

I had always been leery of psychics and their purported abilities. If you're raised as a Christian, as I was, you're likely to be warned to stay away from that kind of thing—and with good reason, if you don't know

---

[3] *Chakras*, meaning "wheels" in Sanskrit, are subtle energy centers in the body.

how to protect yourself. There's no guarantee every psychic is channeling positive energies. So I've relied on my training and experience as an investigator to help me sort things out.

In C3, you learn how to channel for other people. You have three 20-minute sessions a week with different people, and then you come back to class and discuss them. The sister of someone in my C3 class had had cancer for quite a few years and was dying. The woman in my class asked the rest of us in the group whether or not her sister could be healed. I was so shocked at the answer I got from Raphael—a definite *no*—that I waited until after the class to talk with her privately. I told her Raphael had been extremely clear. He said her sister had had many extensions of life, but now her soul was resisting and didn't want any more. Her soul wanted to return, to go back. I think I was the first person to say that to her directly, but other people later confirmed the message I'd gotten from Raphael. The woman's sister died a few months later.

By then, word started getting out that I had some kind of healing ability, so I found myself doing a lot of 20-minute healing sessions for other people. I knew some healing was taking place just as it had with Carmen that first time, but right from the beginning I was aware it wasn't me, Wayne, who was doing the healing. I'm a channel or a vessel for the pure, positive, and loving healing energies that come through me. In order to work with these energies, I have to prepare myself and call in the guides and the angels. I don't—and can't—do it by myself.

Releasing Entities

At the end of each channeling class, before we leave to go home, everyone stands up and holds hands in a circle while the teacher asks for protection and cleansing. After our session during Passover week, the person on my left told me afterward that when we were holding hands, she felt a loud roar, and then a surge of energy raced up her arm and into her chest. I hadn't felt a thing, but she believed she had an entity inside her and asked me if I would help her release it. I really didn't think I could do anything. It wasn't that I didn't believe in the existence of such entities; I never doubted they were real. But the idea that I could remove them had never crossed my mind. But I wanted to help her if I could, so I made an appointment with her.

Before our scheduled appointment, I had a channeling session with another woman, Maria, whose story is detailed in my previous book *Are You Possessed?* Maria grew up impoverished and suffered physical and emotional abuse. She had been struggling for years to find and maintain a connection with the Divine, only to repeatedly fall back into a state of despair. During my session with her, it became abundantly clear to me that removing or releasing these entities was exactly the form of healing my guides were training me to do.

This particular session, which took place the day after the channeling class on the first day of Passover, was my third with Maria. In our first two sessions, I'd witnessed some sudden and dramatic changes take place in her voice, in her eyes, and in her language. I'd already realized that behavior wasn't coming from *her*. It was coming from something inside her, some type of entity. So during our third session, I intentionally provoked the entity. As soon as it made its presence known, I looked directly into Maria's eyes and said, "This is Wayne you're talking to!" I don't know why I said that. I just wanted to help her. And it worked, at least for the moment. The entity retreated, and Maria was herself again.

But as we were embracing when she was about to leave, I sensed the entity was active again. Although I didn't know why, I was led to glide her arms to her side and pick her up in a bear hug, so I did. As I pulled her up onto the balls of her feet, I called on Jesus, Archangel Michael, and Archangel Raphael. I just kept repeating their names, "Jesus, Michael, Raphael." Maria said she could feel the energy radiating from her feet. She sensed the pure energy of love and light.

I didn't understand all of it, and I still don't; but somehow I knew what was going on, even that very first time. I wasn't frightened or upset by what was happening. It didn't feel foreign or strange to me. I felt like I had done it before. Where does that come from? I'm not sure myself.

Maria left the session floating on a cloud, but I soon realized the entity was loose in my house, attempting to get to me through my auric shield. Since that experience, I have learned how extremely important it is to maintain a strong auric shield. (See Chapter 12 for more information on the auric shield.) I called on the angels, and two of them escorted the entity into the heavens, removing it from the planet so it wouldn't be able to return to harm Maria or anyone else ever again. I learned a valuable lesson from that potentially dangerous situation. Simply removing an entity is not enough. You have to send it to the Light *immediately*. The Light is Source, God, heaven, home. It's where we come from and where we'll eventually return. Once an entity is sent to the Light, it, too, is where it belongs.

When I finally met with my C1 classmate, she told me she had encountered her entity while driving home the evening after our channeling class. She believed it had a malevolent intelligence that did not want to come in contact with me or my guides. It was not ready to be evicted. Nevertheless, I asked my guides for protection for both of us, and I invited in Jesus, Raphael, and Michael to remove the entity. While I held my left hand on her back, Michael and Raphael pushed and pulled the entity—who did not go willingly—out of her body and took it to the Light. Jesus then entered her to fill her with love and light.

I'm guided in these healing sessions as to where to move my hands or where to place them. Sometimes I have a sense of what's going on with the person I'm working with because I can feel major energetic blocks, which feel like crystallized bricks that need to be broken up and dissolved. But it's when my hands go up to the back of a person's head that my left arm really starts shaking. It feels like electricity going through my hands. Usually the other person can feel it, too. It's a shock, kind of like the nerve stimulation you get using a tens unit.

As strange as it sounds, the message I get about what's happening is that neurotransmitters are being reconfigured. Neurotransmitters that aren't beneficial are being shut off, and new pathways are being rebuilt.

Since those two healings, I've occasionally worked with other guides, but Archangel Raphael, Archangel Michael, and Jesus are always present. Raphael is a powerful healer of people and of animals. I don't see him, but I sense him positioned behind me. When I'm working, his energy merges with mine and goes through me and my hands. I'm a conduit for that healing energy; it's almost as if we're one. Raphael and Michael work together to release entities, and other angels then escort them to the Light. Michael, who is a leader among the archangels, a warrior who provides protection and liberates us from fear and negativity, is usually positioned in front of me, to my left. Raphael and Michael act from the outside to push and pull the entities out. Jesus, who is positioned in front of me to my right, actually goes inside. He is the only one who goes in, but he won't do it unless the person gives permission. Jesus always fills the person with love and light.

But what about Athena, who originally came through as one of my three main guides? Time and time again in the course doing these healings, I asked her, "Do you want in on this?" Her answer was always, "No." But if she was one of my guides, why wasn't I sensing her? Why wasn't she participating in the healings? I wondered if she might be there just to provide some feminine energy. But whatever her purpose was, why didn't she make herself known to me? What was she waiting for?

Chapter 2
Discarnates and Demons

Becoming Possessed

When 22-year-old Joanne first came to see me, some of her close friends had moved away, her mother had recently died, and then her elderly neighbor, Betty, died, too. Joanne and her husband weren't close to Betty, but they had been helping her out during her final illness. Almost immediately after Betty passed away at home in her apartment, Joanne began hearing a masculine-sounding voice in her head. The voice told her she hated Jesus and she hated God. It told her she hated her husband, her dog, her life. It claimed she hated everything except Satan. The voice also told Joanne she was scared, which was certainly true, especially since it insisted it would never leave her.

Hearing voices is one of the more revealing signs and symptoms of entity possession. Seeing disturbing or violent mental images, feeling suicidal, and undergoing sudden changes in your disposition or personality, especially following surgery or a traumatic event are some other indicators.

But symptoms of possession are not always dramatic or sudden. Any of the following conditions or incidents *may* be connected with or the result of possession:

- depression

- nightmares

- night terrors

- panic or anxiety attacks

- chronic fatigue or exhaustion

- poor memory or concentration

- addictions and impulsive behavior

- sexual acting out

- migraines

- multiple personality/dissociative disorders

- chronic relationship problems

- spiritual stagnation

In the first of several healing sessions with Joanne, I discovered that Betty had not crossed over after she had died. Her soul was still present on the earthly plane, and it was now *in* Joanne. Betty was afraid, too. While she was alive, she had been possessed by a demon who told her she would be punished for being a bad person. When she died, she looked for somewhere to go to avoid going to hell, and she found Joanne, whose auric shield had already been weakened by her mother's death and the loss of her close friends.

But in spite of what an entity's voice may tell you, being possessed does not mean you are a bad or evil person. There are many different ways you can encounter an entity. You can simply be in the wrong place at the wrong time; you can become temporarily vulnerable, as Joanne had; or you can inadvertently do something that opens the door, so to speak, and lets the entity in. Engaging in certain activities or being in certain places can put you at greater risk for coming in contact with entities. Some things to be careful of include:

- using oracular tools (Ouija board, tarot cards, automatic writing, etc.) without knowing what you're doing or without being protected

- channeling without the proper training or protection

- holding onto strong negative emotions, such as grief, fear, anger, anxiety, or pain

- having surgery or dental work

- spending time in hospitals or cemeteries

- dabbling with black magic or being around someone else who is using black magic

- drinking alcohol or using drugs excessively

This doesn't mean that every time you have surgery, feel anxious, visit a cemetery, or go to a bar you will automatically become possessed by an entity. It means these situations make you more susceptible, especially if you are in a weakened state with a lower vibration or are not adequately protected, which was the case with Joanne.

My work has been a constant learning experience for me, and I expect it will continue to be. When I first began encountering these entities, my impression was that they were easy to acquire, but I have since learned that if you stay positive and strong, you may be attacked, but your risk of possession will be much less than it would be if your vibration is at a low level. (You can learn more about vibration and protection in Chapter 12.)

You can also attract an entity by unwittingly allowing it in, which often happens when someone is unwilling to let go of a close loved one who has died.

When Betty entered Joanne, she wasn't intending her harm, she was seeking her help. Joanne actually heard her ask for it. But whether or not discarnates *intend* harm to their hosts, possession by a discarnate always *results* in harm to both the entity and the host. The natural progression when we die is for our soul to go to the Light. Discarnates do not belong on this plane, and there is nothing positive they can gain or contribute by remaining earthbound.

With the aid of my guides, I assisted Betty in leaving Joanne and going to the Light. During that healing session, Betty apologized to Joanne for the pain she'd caused her. She hadn't known where else to go, and she'd believed Joanne was someone who would be able to find a way to help her. It turned out she was right.

Discarnates

Discarnate beings like Betty are the entities I had been reading about in Edith Fiore's book *The Unquiet Dead* in the incident related in the Introduction. Discarnates are individuals who were formerly alive, but when they die, instead of going directly to the Light, these displaced souls remain on the earthly plane, which is why they are also called earthbound spirits. There are lots of different reasons why discarnates remain here. They may be confused and not realize they have died, especially if their death was sudden. They may be afraid of what comes next, especially if they fear going to hell, as Betty did. Some are motivated to remain here by their attachments, either positive or negative, to people or places—very often to people who are grieving and don't want to lose contact with their lost loved ones.

Once discarnates get into people, they get stuck and can't get out. Usually, all I have to do is show them the Light. I simply say, "Look up." When they see the Light, they know what to do, and they go. Sometimes their deceased loved ones appear to them to encourage them to leave. There are psychics who can actually see discarnates, but I generally feel them rather than see them. Most of the time, as soon as a discarnate leaves and goes to the Light, I experience an immediate back-flash of love from it. It's a love you don't normally experience on this planet, a supernatural love. There's so much appreciation and gratitude that I almost always shed a few tears. It's that powerful and intense.

Not all discarnates attach themselves to living people; some are ghosts who roam around a house or some other building or area without entering and possessing a person. Sometimes these discarnates stay in one location, but other times they may go from place to place with the people they're connected to. Some people I've talked to have had discarnates following them around for 20 years or more. The people know the discarnates are there but assume they just have to keep living with them.

When a discarnate attaches itself to a living person's energy field or aura, or to the person's physical, emotional, or subtle body, it has to be released or it could remain with the host until the person dies. The longer an entity has been in residence, the more likely the host is to believe the entity's agenda is his or her own agenda. That's why the period of time immediately after an entity is removed can be very confusing.

Divine Healings, which transcend time and space, work on four levels: physical, mental, emotional, and spiritual. You receive healing not only for what you carry from this incarnation, but also from what you carry from other lifetimes as well. It may take a while to process everything. And sometimes we can't safely release all of it at once, which is why Divine Healings are most effective over the course of three sessions during a six-week period.

Although it is possible to have only a single entity, once one has gotten in, it is much easier for other entities to get in, too. More often than not, there are multiple entities possessing a single host, each with its own personality and its own agenda. One says, "Do this." Another says, "Do that." A third wants to send you in yet a different direction. I've seen people who have had entities for most of their lives, some since they were young children. They have no idea what it's like to *not* have to listen to a myriad of demanding voices telling them what's wrong with them and what they should do.

Joanne was fortunate, in a way, because she had been free of entities until her neighbor died, so she knew right away that something was very wrong.

Demons

After Betty left Joanne and went to the Light, it became clear that Betty's demon had also found a host in Joanne and had likely caused Betty's spirit to enter her. That demon was the source of the voice Joanne was hearing, and it did more than talk to her. Sometimes it growled, and when it growled, even her husband heard it.

During one of our healing sessions, I called in the protection of a hundred thousand angels and invited my guides in. They removed the demon from Joanne, but she continued to hear the voice—or at least *a* voice. We discovered there were other demons present in her apartment, as well as inside that entire apartment building. Like discarnates, demons don't always attach themselves to a host but sometimes roam around inside or outside buildings. Joanne said that a friend who lived in the same complex had also been hearing voices, as had some of the other residents. After that session with Joanne and her husband, I drove to their apartment. When I arrived, she told me the voice had said it hated me.

Of course, it hated me! Entities feed on your power and energy, and they don't want to be evicted. They'll do and say almost anything to keep from leaving. They know when you've made the choice to be healed, and they will do whatever they can to prevent you from following through. The first thing they'll do is ridicule the idea that entities exist and therefore the idea that anyone could actually release them. "Oh, that's nonsense," they'll say. "That's ridiculous. It's a bunch of hooey." Next, they may threaten you or put obstacles in your way to try to keep you from seeking help, such as physical pain or illness, an empty gas tank, road construction—anything to slow you down or prevent you from taking steps to get rid of them. If you persist and make an appointment to see me, they will often then engage and try to attack *me*. That's why I begin the healing process even before your appointment in order to neutralize the entities and even release some of them and to call on the angels and my guides to protect both of us.

Discarnates and demons don't serve any positive purpose whatsoever. They don't ask your permission or wait for you to invite them in. They're present whether or not you want them there because free will doesn't mean anything to them. And they won't leave at your polite request. Joanne's demons harassed her, intimidated her, and lied to her. They did their best to wear her down on every level, sometimes talking to her nonstop for days at a time.

What's the nature of this demonic or dark-force energy? Where does it come from? There's no way to prove this—and maybe it's because of my Christian background that I see it this way—but I think demons are the fallen angels, the ones who sided with Satan when he rebelled against God. They are still rebelling, still trying to poison the well, causing suffering wherever they go. Demons are much more powerful than discarnates, and there are a lot of them. I estimate there are multiple demons for each person on the planet. Unlike discarnates, demons were not formerly human, so they don't usually have a prior connection with their hosts. Most of them are just looking for an accessible person to use. They are 100% evil and destructive, and they're trying to take down as many of us as they can. Demons are a form of energy. You can't destroy energy; all you can do is transform it.

Where demons come from is less interesting to me than what happens to them when they're sent to the Light. I believe they really are transformed—rehabilitated, if you will. Although they are a form of energy, they are souls, too. I think they see the Light as being their demise, their end—and it's true that once they go to the Light they can't come back to earth—but it's far from the end for them.

After my guides did a house-cleaning at Joanne's apartment complex, she came back to see me, still hearing a voice. She was convinced her demon had returned. But if it had gone to the Light, how could it have returned? I had never encountered anything like that. During this second session, the voice Joanne heard proclaimed himself to be her eternal lover. He was exceedingly jealous of her husband and told Joanne she *belonged* to him. She was his. Furthermore, he claimed Joanne wanted him with her, and in fact, kept calling him back to her—not consciously, of course, but unconsciously. Another healer present at this session is psychic. She said that when my guides had sent that demon to the Light, he told Joanne, "I'll get you. I'm coming back."

During another session, we learned that in a past life Joanne had been involved with a magician—a sorcerer who was in league with some very dark forces. He and Joanne had indeed been lovers. He'd practiced black magic during the time of King Arthur, and Joanne had been one of his students. In another lifetime together, when they were both killed during the Crusades, he'd made a pact with the dark forces to continue to be with Joanne. They gave him the power to rematerialize over and over again, and in each new life, when Joanne called him back, he always returned to her. His intention was to create so much confusion in her mind that she would no longer be able to function in this dimension.

At this point, I wasn't aware of demon-controlled discarnates, so the story we were getting was a little garbled, as is sometimes the case. We were being misled to believe there was only one demon, and that he had the power to return after being taken to the Light. But that was not true.

Cords

Although we didn't yet know how many demons and discarnates we were dealing with, we knew there were some powerful energetic connections—or cords—between Joanne and these entities that still hadn't been severed. Cords are like etheric umbilical cords. They can attach to you at any place on your body, generally at the location of one of the chakras, typically in your chest area where the heart chakra is located. Cords can connect you to a person, a place, or a thing either in this life or in a past life. About half the cords I've seen are connected to people who are still alive. Cords are not always negative or harmful. We often have energetic cords between ourselves and our loved ones, for example. Sometimes those cords are positive and sometimes they're not. If they're harmful, they need to be cut because they can affect you in a lot of different ways.

When I'm working with someone who has cords, I don't necessarily know where they all go (what's on the other end), and I don't need to know that. What's important is cutting them, if they're harmful, and being done with them so you don't have to deal with those issues anymore. Cords are like weeds. If you chop a weed off at the topsoil level but don't get rid of the roots, it can quickly grow back. In order to get rid of cords completely, we have to not only cut them, we also have to pull their roots out of the person's body. Many people I've worked with have actually felt the etheric roots of their cords being pulled out of them.

I asked Archangel Michael to cut every cord that was connecting Joanne to any and all dark entities. Those cords were conduits that had been allowing the dark energy to return to her again and again over hundreds and hundreds of years. After we began cutting them, Joanne started hearing numbers. Archangel Michael was telling her how many past-life cords she had. The final number was 182! And he cut every one of them. When he finished cutting them, he sent them to the Light so their energy would not be left to float around on this planet, and Joanne finally stopped hearing the demonic voice. After so many lifetimes, the connection had finally been severed.

What the guides tell us is that whether something has happened in the past, will happen in the future, or is happening right now, it's actually *all* happening right now. That's a hard concept for me to get my mind around, but if it's true, it would explain why all of Joanne's past lives were affecting her in the present.

Attachments

Joanne told me that when she first came to see me she was distraught and depressed. I remember our first few sessions when she couldn't even sit still in her chair. A month later, she was much calmer and more in control of herself. She was no longer hearing the voice all the time and she no longer had any demons inside her. At that point, with the presence of so many guides around her, it would have been very, very difficult for anything else to get into Joanne. But although she did not have any entities in her, she was still being attacked by demonic attachments, which, in her case, were related to more past-life issues.

Unlike entities, attachments do not get into you to possess you. They get through your auric shield when you're weak and latch onto you on the outside. Like leeches or ticks, they can suck the life force right out of you. They can actually make you feel sick, the same as demons can. They're similar to demons and just as prevalent. The bigger danger with attachments is that they tend to weaken you further. They can fracture your auric shield and make you vulnerable to stronger, more invasive entities. The only agenda attachments have is survival; basically, they're parasites. They work on you physically, mentally, emotionally, and spiritually. If you don't get rid of attachments, they can create all kinds of problems. They are nearly as destructive as demons and should be treated with the same caution.

There are a lot of different theories about where attachments come from and what they are, and the psychics and healers who can actually see them can sometimes detect where they come from. Some people may be interested in obtaining that kind of information, but again it's not my bailiwick. I don't focus on where they come from because I think it's more important to remove them so they stop harming people.

Treating the Symptoms

It was no surprise Joanne's doctors believed she was schizophrenic. One of them prescribed an antipsychotic, and another put her on anti-anxiety medication. So many people visit medical practitioners and psychiatrists for their physical, mental, and emotional problems, but regardless of the diagnosis and treatment, they don't experience any relief or healing because the underlying source of the problem is still there. These people continue to live unhappy, sometimes tormented lives for years. You have to wonder what percentage of people in jail and mental hospitals are there because they're possessed. What would our world look like if they were effectively healed? Obviously not all blocks, problems, and illnesses are the result of possession, but many of them definitely are. And when the source of the problem is entity possession, most doctors or therapists are powerless to provide a cure.

Often by the time people come to see me they have already been through the gamut of medical doctors, drugs, hospitalizations, psychiatric treatments, etc. Coming to me may be their last resort. But after the entities have been removed, they are then able to respond to whatever medical and/or psychological treatment they need because they are no longer dealing with someone else's agenda. They're able to do their own work and learn how to take care of themselves.

While entity removal is often the key element in someone's path back to wellness, it isn't a panacea or a quick fix. Results are not 100%, and not everyone is 100% better instantly. Sometimes that *is* the case. Many people can feel the entities leaving them, and they say they feel lighter. That's the most common report I get. But healing is a gradual process. No matter how much better you feel in the short term, after a healing you have to make long-term lifestyle changes and changes in your thinking; otherwise, you're going to be susceptible to possession again. Although the entities that were removed can't return, more are always lurking around waiting for an opportunity. It's just like being healed from a physical illness or disease. If you resume the bad habits that led to the illness, you're likely to get sick again. So what you do after a Divine Healing to change your negative thinking and raise your vibration to protect yourself is as important as what I can do for you.

Over the course of several Divine Healing sessions, Joanne became stronger and calmer. She started to get in touch with her own guides, especially Archangel Gabriel, who often comes through to me and who came through every time I worked with Joanne. She learned to call on Gabriel to request his protection and was able to recognize his presence. He had been with her all along, but she hadn't been aware of him, just as Raphael had been with me all those years without my knowing it. From then on, she was able to call on Gabriel and her other guides whenever she felt she needed protection.

After what she'd been through, it wasn't surprising that the biggest obstacle Joanne had to overcome was her own fear. That's true for so many people. Although she continued to struggle with her fear, she got better and better at dealing with it. She learned how to counter negative thoughts with positive ones. She developed a more positive attitude and raised her overall vibrational level. By calling on and using her guides regularly, she kept herself protected. When I saw Joanne six weeks after our first session, she was not the same person who had first come to see me. She was transforming her fear through love.

Experiencing a Divine Healing

The Divine Healing process utilizes the energy of Jesus Christ and the angelic and archangelic realms. It works on four levels: physical, mental, emotional, and spiritual. Only love and light are transferred to you during a Divine Healing. Most of the work takes place on another plane or dimension, so it is not painful. While some people report feeling physical sensations such as pressure, heat, lightness, or a jerking movement, you may not even be aware of what is being done on your behalf.

Each person's situation is somewhat unique in terms of the long-term healing process, but a couple of things are true for everyone. After a Divine Healing session, you will definitely need to take extra-good care of yourself as your body cleanses the remaining toxicity and energetic debris at the pace that is best for you. Drinking lots of pure water is essential. You will have received energetic assistance to help you move your life forward, but this is not a passive process. You will need to pay close attention to your thoughts and your behavior. When you notice you are thinking or acting negatively, you *can* intervene and turn your thoughts and behavior in a positive direction. It's hard enough to deflect all the negativity we're bombarded with on a daily basis from TV, radio, the internet, and the newspapers. It's next to impossible to turn your thoughts in a positive direction if you've got one or more entities inside you. They just keep you down no matter what you do. But once you are free of them and their influence on you, it's much easier to raise your vibrational frequency and stay on the positive side.

Many healers or spirit releasement practitioners believe you have to engage with an entity prior to releasing it, so they get into a dialogue with it to coax it into agreeing to leave. I don't do that. I don't engage them at all; in fact, they engage me. It isn't necessary to get them to agree to go. If something negative is there, my guides remove it right away.

The same is true of karma. What you've done or not done in a past life may have set you up for possession in this lifetime, as was the case with Joanne, but you don't need to know the details in order to be healed. Focusing on going back into your past lives to find an explanation isn't necessary. What we need to do is address *what* is happening right now, rather than *why* it's happening. If you want to delve into your past lives to explore them, there are other people you can turn to for help who are experts in that area. I don't need that information in order to do removal and healing.

I know of several cases where people have tried various means to get rid of entities, such as prayer to God or the angels, priests, and exorcisms, but none of it had any effect. I'm not sure what forces were at work in those situations that prevented the entities from being removed then, or why my guides and I were subsequently able to help. There's a lot I don't yet know, but I trust that my guides will always let me know enough at any given time to do what needs to be done.

More than three-quarters of the people I work on now aren't consciously aware of what I'm doing because the healing is being done remotely, usually at the request of a close friend or loved one. In those cases, the person isn't able to give me permission to do the work, but the person's higher self gives permission. I can communicate with them soul-to-soul, and whenever I've done that, the soul has always given me permission.

I also work remotely on residences, cleaning house, if you will. Once an entire family came to see me, leaving only their daughter's 19-year-old boyfriend at home, and during the session, I went into their house remotely to clean in. I didn't know he was in there, and he had no idea what I was doing. While I was working on the house, the young man suddenly saw a black shadow; then the family cat began running around up and down the stairs and all over the house. The young man fled in a hurry. He later said God had told him to get out of there. In spite of the fact that after the cleaning the house felt clear, good, and much lighter to everyone else—and even the cat had calmed down—it took a couple of months before he would venture back inside.

Quite a few of the people who come to see me turn out to have psychic or healing abilities they had not been aware of. That was the case with Joanne, who at the end of her six weeks was just beginning her journey of exploring and understanding the extent of her abilities in these areas. Entities are drawn to people who are doing this kind of work. Sometimes they're going for the strength, energy, and power of the person, to try to take it over and use it for their own purposes. They also want to stop people from releasing entities. If they can lower someone's vibration and transform positive thoughts and energy to negative, they might be able to keep that person from doing the work. But when they target someone who isn't yet fully awake to his or her abilities and the experience is what actually wakes that person up, possession kind of backfires on those entities. It's still a win-win situation in the end because the entities get to go to the Light, which is the best possible place for them. The Light is more powerful than the darkness. Light always transforms darkness.

Although I say "I" do this healing for the sake of conversation or convention, I know it isn't me who's doing the actual healing. I serve as a channel or a vessel for spirit. I have the ability to call in the angels and the guides, and they're the ones who remove the entities. They're the ones who do the healing through me. When the angels and the guides are present, I feel their energy flowing through me, especially through my hands, and I know how to do whatever needs to be done.

When other people with different abilities are present with me, we're all doing the healing together. It's a shared experience. Each person brings something unique, a different sensibility, a different approach. There have been times when I've been extremely grateful to have had other healers present—times when it required the combined efforts of several of us to understand and deal with what we were all seeing and sensing. If these other people hadn't been there experiencing the same things I was experiencing, I might not have trusted my own senses.

PART TWO

Chapter 3
The "Guests" Who Refused To Leave

Hearing Carl's Story

"I feel like I'm half dead," Carl said. "Like I'm not really present." He wasn't exaggerating about how discouraged he felt. By the time he came to see me, Carl had considered ending his life.

He had been referred to me by another healer who told him he had an attachment, but he had been seeking help from medical practitioners, alternative healers, and psychics for numerous physical and psychological problems for the better part of two decades—almost entirely without relief. His allergist told him he was the "most allergic" patient he'd ever seen. He was born and grew up in Illinois, but when he was in high school his family sent him to a boarding school in Santa Fe for a year because his allergies were so severe they thought he might die. As a result of the Southwest's dry air, higher altitude, and lower levels of pollen, he got much better during the course of that year and was able to return to Illinois to finish high school. He moved back to New Mexico when he was 17.

In addition to allergies, Carl also suffered from asthma and chronic fatigue syndrome, and he had been born with severe eczema that went into remission when he was in his 30s. The eczema returned more than 20 years ago and had become especially debilitating in the last 12 to 15 years. He described the condition as a "torment" that was equal to or worse than all his other symptoms combined, which included heavy post-nasal drainage that led to severe stomach problems.

A practitioner Carl had been treating with a decade or so ago believed mercury was the root of his health issues, so Carl tried to have all the fillings removed from his teeth. The practitioner gave him what he said was a very small dose of something that resulted in most of Carl's body swelling. He remembered being nearly delirious for a week afterward, and it was several years before he began to recover from that treatment.

Carl believed the eczema was genetic because his father and his father's siblings had all had childhood eczema, as had his paternal grandmother. His brother, who had died two years earlier of an alcohol-related accident, also suffered from it, although their younger sister did not have any allergies or skin problems.

I felt that I was in Carl's energy field even before he arrived for his first session. Once he got there, my guides communicated a sense of urgency, so I said a prayer for protection, and the guides began working on him right away. I could sense Carl had something in him with an agenda, and it did not want to go. In the first round, we removed two demons and a discarnate. We removed another discarnate a short while later. While we were removing the entities from Carl, I had the impression his mother, who had died nine years earlier, was present. She was sending her son love and reassurance and letting him know she and other loved ones had helped direct him to this healing.

I couldn't tell exactly how long the four entities had been with Carl, but it had been a long time—long enough that one or more of them could have been related to a past life. It was also possible some of his health issues were the result of the discarnates we had removed.

When people die and do not go to the Light, they often retain whatever medical or psychological problems or, in the case of a drug or alcohol abuser, any cravings they may have had at the time of their death. So when a discarnate with any of these conditions enters someone, that person, the host, can then begin manifesting the same, or similar, problems. If one of the discarnates in Carl had skin-related issues and one had allergy issues, they could have brought those problems to him. If that was the case, while medications might be able to alleviate the symptoms somewhat, they wouldn't be able to resolve the underlying issues.

Carl's body had taken quite a beating, and his continuing poor health and depression only made him more open to possession. He acknowledged that at one time he drank heavily, which is another good way for entities to get in. As a result of all these factors, his auric field had been shattered. He would need to learn how to strengthen it and keep it strong.

I told Carl not to expect immediate results. His energy had been completely depleted; he had no energetic resources left. The next six weeks would be critical for him, as they are for anyone who has had entities removed. He would be undergoing a major detox physically, emotionally, mentally, and spiritually, and I advised him to drink as much water as possible during the next 72 hours in order to help dissolve and release any remaining particles of negativity that were left. I also told him Jesus would stay inside him for the next two or three days to help him process what had happened. I reminded him that although his thoughts were no longer controlled by the entities we had removed, some of those negative patterns would still be with him. He would need to work on noticing and changing them over time. But at least now he had the ability to make choices.

My guides let me know the work we had done was all Carl could handle at that time but that other entities might still be inside him.

Carl agreed to come back for two or three additional sessions over the next few months. Just then his mother came through again to say, "Yes, you have to come," which made both of us chuckle. She had died and gone to the Light, but she was still being a mother.

Before he left, Carl asked about his house. He didn't see the point of returning to a house "full of negative stuff," which he assumed was the case since he had been living there for 15 years and had had so much negativity in him. I went into his house remotely with my guides, and they found and removed several entities. I asked the guides to cleanse and protect the house and to cleanse and protect both Carl and me.

Bringing a Healing Team Together

While Carl had come to me for help and sincerely wanted to be healed—or at least to experience some relief from his debilitating symptoms—he had been suffering for so long and had seen so many different healers and practitioners he was skeptical that removing these entities would really do him any good.

Nevertheless, based on what I'd seen with so many other people, I expected good results from his healing. He attempted to contact me after our session, but we played phone tag for several weeks during which time I didn't see him again. From his messages, I gathered he was not experiencing much improvement, and since that's not the norm, it kind of baffled me. Only about 3-5% of people who have the kind of healing he had claim to have no response from it. Because he didn't come in for another session, I wasn't sure what to do or what was going on with him.

Then one day I was at a Whole Foods grocery store with my friend, Lisa, who is a psychic, and we saw Carl in the parking lot. His situation had been puzzling me, so I'd already told her a little bit about him, but she'd never met or seen him before. I didn't even have the opportunity to point him out before she noticed him. Spirit started giving her information about him right then and there, telling her Carl had some kind of an alien or reptilian possession. As Carl got out of his car and went into the store, Lisa actually saw him as a reptile. That really scared her. She didn't want to have anything to do with him. He was really scurrying, too. You wouldn't think someone who is so disabled could scurry, but that's what he was doing.

I had a conversation with him before leaving the grocery store and told him what Lisa had observed. He said no one had ever mentioned anything like that to him before. But even as we were talking, I sensed the presence of someone or something else. Carl would be looking out at me through *his* eyes, and then he would blink very slowly, and the eyes looking at me were *not his*. Those other eyes were mocking me; they were telling me there was nothing I could do to them.

Later, I asked Lisa and Robert, another fellow healer, to meet with Carl and me, not necessarily to do any type of healing, but to explore his situation to see if there was something we could do for him later on. Lisa was still afraid, but she trusted me to protect her. So the next time Carl and I met, she and Robert joined us. In the meantime, since his last session with me, Carl had been to see the person who had referred him to me, and she had told him he still had three entities inside him. She also told him there was some sort of an alien communication device, which she referred to as a "transistor," that had been implanted in him a long time ago and was still there.

During this second session, Carl's mother again made her presence known. Through Lisa, she explained that the possession Carl was dealing with actually went back as far as three previous generations, to Carl's paternal great-grandfather. The purpose of it—*at least as it was revealed to us then*—was to transmit secrets and ancient wisdom from an alien race. These alien beings were somehow going to be able to retrieve the information from Carl by means of the device inside of him.

Lisa first saw the three entities as reptilian but very humanoid looking. She said they were able to conceal their reptilian traits. They presented themselves to us as benign and loving "Star Beings" that had crash-landed on this planet several generations ago but had no intention of harming or dominating anyone. Their interest was in the minerals "rich within the earth." Being unable to get home, they had taken up residence in Carl's ancestor's DNA. Carl and his ancestors were vessels for the survival of the three beings and the information they were safeguarding. Their genes had been mixing with the genes from Carl's paternal bloodline during these three generations.

What was unusual about Carl's situation was that the transistor, or transmitter, appeared to be part of his genetics and not something that had been implanted. The same was true of the alien beings. They hadn't actually entered or come into him; they were intrinsic to him. They had been co-conscious with his ancestors. And since they were part of his DNA, they couldn't be removed in the traditional manner.

The message they conveyed to us was that Carl was a healer and a teacher, and as a result of this multigenerational possession, he had some important wisdom and knowledge within himself that was crucial for him to share with others at this point in time. But there were indications a third-party race also wanted access to this information, in essence turning Carl's body into a battleground in a tug of war.

Carl was less interested in the nature of whatever knowledge he might have within himself, or in sharing it, than he was in simply feeling less miserable. He told us his mother had apologized to him right before she died, and he'd assumed it was because she felt responsible in some way for the miserable conditions of his life. Although Carl believed we choose the circumstances of our lives before we are born, and he told his mother that, he still didn't understand why he and so many other people had to deal with such pain and anguish. Why was anyone born just to suffer so much?

And why would *he* have chosen such difficult circumstances?

The story the healing team put together from our guides and from the three beings was this: Carl's physical and psychological suffering was a result of his soul's agreement to take on the task of revealing the information he carried within himself. The ante was being upped now because this incarnation was the time when he was supposed to reveal it. Did that mean that if he made the choice to go forward to become the teacher and healer he was meant to be his suffering would be alleviated? The answer seemed to be "yes." Carl was willing to try, if only for the chance of regaining his health, but he had no idea how to access the information or what to do next. Nor could we give him detailed instructions on how to proceed or a list of steps to take.

After feeling stymied for so many years, Carl had lost faith in himself. "It scares me," he said, "because I feel like I'm not going to be able to do it."

So he was willing, but he was also fearful and confused. Over the years many different psychics and other practitioners had told him he was a healer and a teacher, and he wondered if the rest of us weren't simply picking that up from him. And yet, in spite of his skepticism, he wanted to believe there was something that could be done to restore his health and allow him to live a normal life.

Unmasking the Reptilians

After that initial group session, Carl met individually with Robert, who did some energy work with him and balanced his chakras. While the two of them were on a guided journey together, three vague hooded figures with their faces concealed appeared to both of them. Assuming these were the three beings who had taken up residence in him, Carl hoped the "guests" would respond when he expressed his willingness to honor his soul's contract. He hoped that after his session with Robert the entities would either leave so he could get well and begin to do his work or at least "pack up" and get ready to go. But that did not turn out to be the case.

The next time the healing team met with Carl, his mother came through to Lisa and told her son the reason he was of such great importance at this time of transformation was because he carried a high percentage of DNA from Star Beings that had been on this plane for hundreds of thousands of years. He was an evolution of the Reptilian gene in that he had a heart, and he had the ability to evolve that "arrangement" (reptilian and human) into something new. His mission was to help others who might have the same genetic make-up to bring it into the world's awareness.

We asked the entities if they had to remain in Carl or if they could leave. Lisa saw three figures she referred to as ancestors. The one in the center was taller, but they were all quite tall—tall and black-hooded. She described them as being "in unity." Although they were able to leave, they were not budging.

They told her they were unwilling to go because they were afraid that without their presence the information Carl carried would be lost. When we asked them if it was their presence within Carl that was making it difficult for him to live a full and joyful life, they became agitated and then downright accusatory. They scolded Carl, telling him what he was experiencing was what he had "signed up for." He had chosen to be the keeper, the protector, and he needed to fulfill his mission. In order to do that, he had to write.

Well, first of all, Carl was not a writer. How could he undertake such an enormous task when he was still ill? Carl and I both wanted to know the answer to that question. Secondly, if his health needed to improve before he could begin accessing this information and putting it into writing—and in order for his health to improve the "guests" needed to leave—why were they refusing to depart?

The largest of the three beings appeared to try talking one of the other two into going, supposedly as an act of compromise. However, no one was willing to leave, and their discussion devolved into arguing. Carl said their bickering reminded him of what went on inside his head. He wondered if the stress and frustration he'd been experiencing for so many years, which his father had also experienced, was related to having these three beings present.

As soon as the arguing commenced, the entities' story—and their benevolent façade—quickly fell apart. Lisa saw an orb connected to Carl's energy body that she said not even Jesus could penetrate. And my guides told me that this was *not their dominion*. But why couldn't Jesus get through the orb? Why didn't he or Michael or Raphael have dominion over these three?

Carl was not the first person with whom this had happened. There were four or five other people I'd worked with before him where Jesus, Michael, and Raphael just stood there and would not do anything. I didn't understand it. We had work to do for those other people, too, but my guides wouldn't go in. Then one day when I was riding my bike, pushing pretty hard on it, Jesus came through to me and said, "I don't have dominion." That just blew my mind. As someone who considers himself a born-again Christian, I was totally baffled by that.

At that time, the only explanation I was given was that Jesus, Michael, and Raphael are here to help the human beings on this earth plane. They may be tapped in with the One God, but this universe is vast. Of course, that explanation raised more questions than it answered, and I wanted greater clarification. But I had already learned I need to practice patience in order to do this work.

We continued to try to talk to the three beings, but when we suggested Carl had the right to exercise his free will and decide whether or not he wanted them with him—which he unequivocally did not— they became even more agitated. I told them it was time for them to move on to a new life. It was time for them to go to the Light. At that point, they attacked Lisa, who had been trying to communicate and negotiate with them. She told us they energetically grabbed her by the neck and tried to get her to throw herself across the room, all the while warning her to mind her own business. They didn't do anything to me, but at the same time they were attacking Lisa, they began jabbing Robert in the neck, inflicting actual physical pain. They were testing us, pushing and pulling, trying to intimidate us.

It was suddenly abundantly clear to all of us that these beings were not who they claimed to be. They were not loving, not heart-based. Reptilians are not. And as one of the members of the healing team put it, what we were being confronted with was the textbook Reptilian agenda[4].

---

[4] The Reptilian agenda refers to the Reptilians' eons-old attempt to dominate and enslave humanity by using fear, manipulation, and mind-control, and by interbreeding with selected humans to gain positions of power all over the world.

Chapter 4
The Alien Reptilians

Who Are They?

These alien Reptilians are multidimensional extraterrestrials who may have originated in the Alpha Draconis star system, but wherever they come from, they have been plaguing planet Earth for eons. I don't think anyone here knows exactly when they arrived on the planet. Many ancient cultures and religions throughout Europe, Asia, Africa, and the Americas include references to dragons, serpents, and races of reptilian humanoids. My sense is they've been here almost as long the planet has been here. They consider this planet *their* planet. They've been controlling us from Day One, and they consider humans to be no more than cattle or slaves. We're just pawns in their game, and their goal is to use the human race and keep us in bondage. They have infiltrated most of the major power structures—financial, government, media, and military—not just in this country, but all over the world.

I don't believe any more Reptilians are coming to this planet. They've been interbreeding with us all along and they're still breeding and interbreeding. Being multidimensional, they have the ability to shape-shift. When someone has enough of the Reptilian DNA, that person—who is part-human, part-Reptilian (Reptoid)—can shape-shift back and forth between human and Reptilian. But someone has to have a tremendous amount of the Reptilian DNA in order to do that. There are people who have witnessed this shape-shifting, but I haven't seen it.

I think the Reptilians are being exposed now because this planet is in a transition, a positive one, although it may not feel positive to everyone right now. The Reptilians have had control of Earth, but they're losing their control very rapidly. Things may get worse before they get better, but the Reptilians' game is definitely changing. No longer are we going to be their pawns or slaves.

Where Are They?

Most of us have some Reptilian DNA, but it isn't activated in everyone at birth. It may be part of the 90% of our DNA that scientists report is inactive. (Not being a scientist, I don't fully understand all of it, but this is the information I've gotten from my guides.) If someone is born with the Reptilian DNA activated, they are considered to have Reptilians in their bloodline, and by now the Reptilian bloodline is out there in quite a few people. This means the Reptilians are not just standing on the sidelines controlling a particular financial institution, for example. They are *in* and possessing—and in the bloodline of—the high-level financiers, the people at the top. This goes back hundreds or thousands of years, and includes kings and queens, people in monarchies and in other ruling classes. The Reptilians are looking for additional people in order to maintain the bloodline. That's one of the reasons for arranged marriages among the ruling political and wealthy elite families around the globe.

Some individuals actually use their free will to choose the darkness over the Light. They choose to be a part of the Reptilian agenda. I run across them every now and then. I don't understand it. It's spooky.

Just as with discarnates and demons, not all Reptilians are in people. Many of the Reptilians are above ground harassing us, but legions more live underground, where they have nests and portals, their bases of operation. Unlike discarnates and demons, however, the Reptilians don't simply possess someone; they actually alter his or her genetic code[5] by implanting a "homing device." It's not a physical implant, but more like an etheric or energetic chip that keeps the connection active. They alter the genetic code even if they are not in the person's bloodline. But if they are in a person's bloodline, that person will always also have Reptilians in him or her. As I soon discovered, it takes more energy to disable the bloodline and remove the etheric homing device from someone's genetic code than it does to have individual Reptilians removed.

Normally, they possess people in threes, like the three "guests" who were in Carl. You don't have to be a major player in one of the power structures to have Reptilians in you or to have the Reptilian bloodline. Anyone is susceptible. Carl was not in any kind of a powerful position, but maybe he would have been or could have been if he hadn't been born with the Reptilian bloodline. They completely neutralized him; they took him right out of the game of life.

Carl didn't have any children, but if someone is born with the Reptilian bloodline and has children, the children will usually have them, too, and there is a high probability their children will also have them. However, it is possible for it to skip a generation. The bloodline may just follow down the female line or it may follow down the male line—or possibly both—I don't know yet. I've learned that I don't need to understand everything right now. The information is unfolding as I go along, as I need to know it.

How long someone has had Reptilians can make a big difference in the kind of outcome they will have after they are removed. Unfortunately, the people who are born with them and have them for dec-

---

[5] The genetic code is the biochemical basis of heredity in human beings and nearly all other life forms on Earth.

ades have a much more difficult time reprogramming themselves once the Reptilians are removed. Carl, for example, had no idea what life could be like without them. Each Reptilian has an agenda, and they're all whispering in your ear, telling you how to be and what to do. It's the only life you know. Not only can they make you ill, they will block you from connecting with your guides and with Source—with God, if you want to use that term. It's as if they put a lead shield around you that you can't penetrate no matter how hard you try.

That's why I've been continually told to look to the children, to heal the children. They're better able to handle it, and it's much easier for a child to recover than it is for someone who's 40, 50, or 60 years old and has been possessed for decades.

What Do They Want?

Reptilians by nature are malicious and deceitful. If you try to communicate with them, they will blow smoke at you. They will try to convince you they're here for the person's highest and best good, and they're trying to help that person. I'm not aware of any "good" or evolving Reptilians. I'd like to believe they are evolving, and I've heard other people say they are, but if that's the case I haven't encountered any that are. That's not part of my experience, and as far as I'm concerned, it's Reptilian propaganda. They are all negative entities that don't honor universal laws[6] and don't recognize our free will.

Just like demons, the source of their power is the darkness. They have no natural enemies on this planet, no one here who can challenge them. But the Reptilians are far more powerful than even the demons, which they control to a great degree. When I'm doing a healing, the Reptilians usually sacrifice some demons to make me believe I've finished my work. I've gotten much more thorough as I've

---

[6] For an excellent description of the universal laws, I highly recommend *The Light Shall Set You Free* by Dr. Norma Milanovich and Dr. Shirley McCune. It's a book I frequently suggest my clients read.

had more experience with them and have learned how devious they are.

I don't see Reptilians and I don't need to see them, but I know a number of psychics who do have the ability to see these things. It freaks them out to no end, but I give them a lot of credit for having the courage to stay with it. Those who do see them usually see them wearing hoods just like these gang bangers with their dark blue or black hoods. Some people have glimpsed them out of the corner of their eye out in the streets or at the shopping malls or on street corners. They tell me the Reptilians are tall, usually between and eight and ten feet, and ugly—extremely ugly.

They Need to Go!

I'm primarily working with removing the Reptilians because I think they've pretty much taken over things. I don't think there are many Greys[7] left. Maybe a few; but I think whatever battle needed to be won with the Greys has been won. So now the major battle is really with the Reptilians. But I don't see any benefit in thinking about or discussing them other than for the purpose of getting a basic idea of who they are. All I want to do is remove them, decrease their numbers, and send them to the Light.

There is a lot more information about them available in books and on the internet, if you want to go looking for it, but giving them attention just calls them in. It lowers your vibrational frequency. They feed on our fear and negativity. As long as people on this planet are angry and agitated, fighting and killing each other, the Reptilians are happy.

We don't fully understand all of this yet, but Reptilians really do exist. They are energy. They are alive. They have souls. And I would like to believe that somewhere along the line they just got pinched off from Source. So it's my intention that when I send them to the Light they

[7] Grey Aliens, so-called because of their skin color, are from the planet Zeta Reticuli and are also known as Zeta Reticulans. They are the most common extraterrestrials reported to have been seen by alien abductees.

are rehabilitated and cannot return to any planet anywhere to harm other beings ever again. It's a healing for them, too.

I don't like talking about them, nobody does. But the message needs to get out there. They don't want the message to get out. They go to great lengths to prevent it. But power is with the Source and the Light, which are so much stronger. Darkness can't hide from the Light. Darkness is no match for the Light.

I see a lot of beauty in the world. There is a lot to be positive about if that's what you're focused on. So keep focusing on the positive. Keep focusing on love.

Chapter 5
One "Guest" Gets Evicted

Getting a Clearer Picture

Immediately after Lisa had told me she'd seen Carl as a reptile at the Whole Foods store, I did some research and investigation into Reptilians. So by the time the healing team met with Carl for the first time, I already knew a little bit about them.

During Carl's individual session with Robert, he perceived the vague, hooded figures who appeared to him in "kind of a gray mist" (the same thing Lisa saw afterward when we were all together) as being something out of a horror story. But even though the three figures had felt threatening to him, we had all gone into our second group session giving the "guests" the benefit of the doubt as to their identity and purpose.

We'd been misled by what they'd originally told us, which was that they would only leave when Carl honored his agreement to deliver their message. We may also have been led astray by our own previous experiences and preconceptions. Each person is unique. We each believe and disbelieve different things and are better at some things than we are at others. And each person has a filter through which he or she sees and interacts with the rest of the world. This is true for channeling as well. The guides speak through people, using the individuals' own voices and vocabularies. When we are channeling, the information we receive passes through our personal filters. During our sessions, the healing team was receiving information from a lot of different guides, all of which was passing through our own filters.

The Reptilians had been busy blowing smoke at us and were successful in deceiving us in the short term. But in spite of all their efforts to throw us off track, it hadn't taken us long to get them to reveal their true colors. They were not remotely interested in helping or protecting Carl; their only interest was in protecting themselves. That's why they became so agitated when we began questioning them. They finally got caught, and they're not used to getting caught.

Unmasking the Reptilians only strengthened our resolve to try to help Carl, but this was new territory for us, and we needed to tread carefully. It was also a tremendous learning experience, and I'd felt from the beginning that the team had come together both to help Carl and to learn. Carl, on the other hand, was anxious to move things along. Regardless of any prior agreement he may have made, he wanted to have these unwanted guests evicted as soon as possible. He asked us why we couldn't just get the information he was supposedly carrying out of him, but of course we couldn't do that.

He asked, "You've never gotten this from anybody else you ever worked with?" We truthfully answered that we had not.

Although Jesus, Archangel Michael, and Archangel Raphael had made it clear they did not have dominion when it came to dealing with the Reptilians, Lisa and I both sensed during the second group session that there were Star Beings who did have dominion and who would be willing and able to assist us. Neither of us yet knew who those Star Beings were.

The rest of us agreed to communicate with our guides and put our heads together during the following week before getting together with Carl again.

Meeting the Arcturians

I woke up suddenly around three o'clock in the morning the night after that session. I knew something or someone was in the room with me; something was happening. I didn't see anything, but I felt a presence, a peaceful presence. The energy was very positive, very loving. I felt no fear, whatsoever. I just said, "Who's here?" or "Who are you?" And the answer was—not out loud, but telepathically— "Arcturians." *Arcturians? Who are Arcturians?* I asked them what they were doing. They told me they were giving me a download to help me deal with the Reptilians and specifically with Carl. After everything I'd already experienced, I wasn't shocked or surprised. It all felt right. I don't remember everything—there wasn't a lot of conversation—but I gave them my permission to proceed, and the download came through real strong.

I think I had heard someone say they channeled Arcturians before that night, but I had no idea who or what the Arcturians were. The next morning, I started researching them. One thing I found out surprised me, but it also cleared up a mystery. I learned that Athena is the Arcturians' mother ship and that it's in our universe right now helping us. Up till then, I had never understood the purpose of Athena being one of my guides since she had never been involved in any of the work I'd been doing with my other guides, Jesus and Archangel Raphael. I thought she was just that Greek Goddess. But suddenly it made sense. The Arcturians, who are a group consciousness, had set all of this into motion and were waiting for the right time to reveal themselves to me. Just like Raphael, they too had been with me from the beginning. And it was no accident that we were encountering the Reptilians at that particular point in time.

The Arcturians gave the same download to Lisa, and she and I connected with them again during the week. Robert had done his own research on them, so all three of us were better prepared the next time we met with Carl. We had also been in communication with Orion, who had previously told me he would always be here to help and protect us—little did we know from what! He now expressed willingness to participate in the work we were doing.

Before we all gathered together again, I was deep in meditation with the Arcturians, Orion, and God preparing myself for the session, when suddenly I saw one of the Reptilians being hauled away by a group of Arcturians the same way the angels take demons and discarnates. They only took one of the Reptilians—it seemed to be the largest of the three—and he seemed completely incapacitated and dejected. I said, "Take him to the Light, wherever you go, whatever the Light is for the Reptilians." The other two Reptilians became very agitated and concerned as they tried to understand what had just happened. I wasn't sure if I believed what I was seeing, so I asked for confirmation from Raphael and Michael.

I got further confirmation from Carl himself, when he arrived for our session looking more animated and alive than I'd ever seen him. He agreed that he was having one of his best days and that he felt much lighter.

I had asked during my meditation if the other two Reptilians would be going then, too, and the answer was, "No." I was told that would have to be done in stages so Carl could handle it.

During the previous week, all three of us had received similar information concerning Carl. Not only had he been possessed by the three beings, there was something else going on with him. He had a connection with the Reptilians that was at a different level, one that was deeper and much more subtle. It seemed to have something to do with his actual DNA. At that point in this evolving story, we didn't know what to make of that. Needless to say, the more information we received, the more questions we had—questions only the Arcturians could answer.

Robert agreed to channel them at our session, and they confirmed the presence of the transmitter in Carl and described it as a "two-way means of communication," the purpose of which was "subterfuge." They said Carl was unable to take control of his energy field because so much energy was being siphoned off via the transmitter. The Arcturians also confirmed they had removed one of the entities that was interfering with Carl's energy and suggested they might remove the other two Reptilians within the week. Carl would then have the opportunity to "enjoy his energy field for himself," but he would need healing—love, light, and guidance—to assist him in dealing with the after-effects of the removal and to guide him around the rooms of the "mansion" he was living in but had never fully explored or inhabited. The Arcturians were willing to assist, and many angels and archangels were also standing by to be of service. They suggested Carl also call on other healers of his choosing to help him.

Carl had some direct questions for the Arcturians, and they had much more to tell him. They said that as a result of his rich life experiences he would be able to advise and assist others whose situations were similar to his. But, contrary to what the Reptilians had claimed, *Carl was under no obligation to do so.* In fact, he had undergone so much in this lifetime that it would be in his highest good in the short term to simply work on accustoming himself to his new state of being. After that, he could decide how he wanted to proceed. The Arcturians told Carl he would find that he had:

> . . . *a much easier connection with your heart center, through which you connect to your soul energy, and it is through this that you draw down your soul's plan for this life. You will know in your heart what you want to do next. It will feel joyful to you, uplifting and expansive. If it does not, then we would advise you to listen to your heart and not do it.*

This was very good news for Carl, but he wanted to know how long it would take for him to make the adjustment after all the entities were gone. The Arcturians said that in a period of weeks or perhaps a few months, Carl's process of rehabilitation would be between 80 to 90% complete, but that he would continue making small adjustments for the rest of his life.

The Arcturians wanted Carl to know he was surrounded by "many, many beings of Light, both angelic and from higher realms of the star system," who had a great affinity for his energy. Because he now had a sort of blank canvas for much of his energy field, he would be able to draw in what he chose to have. It was a unique opportunity, one that was not frequently presented. Most of all, the Arcturians wanted Carl to know how much he was loved and cherished because of the challenging path he had chosen. They assured him he was overcoming his challenges and reaching a point of culmination.

Acknowledging Carl's Fear

I reminded Carl he was in the process of having a group of entities removed—a group of Reptilian entities—who had an agenda, and who had been with him since birth. They had been making their agenda *his* agenda, so even though they would be gone, his conditioning would still be there. He would continue to think and react in the same way until he realized he didn't need to do that anymore. He admitted that all his life he'd never known what it was like to be "just me." Most people, he said, can figure out what they want to do with their lives, but he'd never had a clue. Even his ability to feel had become deadened.

Many years ago, while standing in the shade of a tree in his backyard, Carl had seen one of his guardian angels. He'd had a few other similar experiences that had led him to believe things were going to start opening up for him then. But it hadn't happened. He thought his fear may have gotten in the way. And as much as everything we were discovering made sense to him, as much as he wanted his suffering to be relieved, and as much as he hoped what the Arcturians were telling him was actually going to happen, that fear was still there.

Maybe that's why his mother had shown up this time.

There had been many times when Carl had come close to ending his life. He told us that just a few months before he had been lying in bed considering suicide, feeling very agonized and praying for help so he wouldn't have to end his life, when he felt a hand across his cheek. It was a sympathetic, loving hand that he felt was trying to comfort him. He wondered if it was his mother's hand. I felt certain it was. I told him that after I'd seen the Arcturians take the first of the three Reptilians during my meditation earlier that day, his mother had come up to me and hugged me.

Carl's ordeal hadn't totally deprived him of his sense of humor. When I told him about his mother hugging me, he laughed and asked, "What's she still doing around here?" I told him she loved him and he acknowledged that was true. It seemed to me his mother had had a hand in directing this process from the very beginning.

Just before ending our session, we gave Carl a healing. Archangel Raphael was present and so were Archangel Michael, Mother Mary, and the Arcturians and Orion, along with many other archangels and angels. Carl's mother was absolutely jumping up and down with joy. So happy. So excited. She was literally dancing.

Before they withdrew, the Arcturians had some words for the healing team. They thanked us for being willing to do the work we were doing and for the love and compassion they saw in us. It was clear to the three of us that we were on a healing journey right along with Carl, who hadn't come to see me by accident. We had started out making no promises or guarantees. We were simply showing up to see if we could offer him some help, yet so much had happened in such a short time. Before the previous session, I had heard of the Arcturians, but I knew nothing about them. Now we were communicating with them and experiencing their power and their strength, as well as their much subtler and higher vibration.

While the process we were involved in hadn't always been fun, it was no doubt a tremendous learning and growing experience. And the Arcturians told me we were not yet done learning and growing from it.

Chapter 6
Arcturians

Our mission is to raise the entire vibrational quality of the planet. What this means is that it is a united effort and many souls all over and within the planet are being introduced to our work.

Dr. Norma Milanovich
We, the Arcturians

Arcturians Among Us

Arcturians are highly-advanced, very loving and peaceful fifth-dimensional extraterrestrials who come from Arcturus, a star in the Boötes constellation. The first person in recent history to mention the Arcturians was Edgar Cayce. After being in communication with them, he wrote that Arcturus was the highest civilization in our galaxy. We didn't know much about them until Dr. Norma Milanovich began channeling them in the 1980s and wrote *We, The Arcturians*, which was published in 1990. Since then, many others have reported being contacted by or having some type of communication with Arcturians, and several books have been published about those experiences.

When they first contacted me, I had heard their name, but I didn't have any idea who they were. Now I'm in communication with them on a daily basis.

The first time I felt their presence around me was in 2010. I was sitting on the patio in front of my house watching the sunset. Suddenly I saw what looked like a funnel cloud, which was odd in itself since we don't get funnel clouds around here, and there were no storms in the area. One part of the "funnel" came out of the cloud, went straight down, and then pointed right at Mt. Taylor, just like a finger pointing.

I felt I was being directed to go to Mt. Taylor, also known as Turquoise Mountain—a place that is sacred to the Navajo and several other Native American tribes—because there was some work for me to do there. A while later as I was driving to the area, I sensed an Arcturian sitting to my right, another one behind me, and a third to my left. Three of them are always with me now and usually in the same positions, although there may be more of them, especially when I'm working. Sometimes they are positioned all the way around me, but there's never one right in front blocking my vision.

The Arcturians are primarily a group consciousness or group soul. Although an individual being may communicate with an individual human on planet Earth, the Arcturian isn't a totally separate individual in the same way the human is a separate person with a unique identity who is disconnected from everyone else. When an Arcturian communicates, that being is communicating from the entire group consciousness rather than from a single limited point of view or experience. So each Arcturian, in a sense, represents all Arcturians. When I was in communication with them initially, it was always with the group consciousness. At times, an individual being may have been "speaking" to me, but until recently I hadn't picked up any specific names. Now I'm regularly in communication with El Morya[8].

The Arcturians communicate telepathically among themselves and with us. Most of what we know about them has come through people who channel them. As I said earlier, each person has a personal filter through which he or she sees and interacts with the rest of the universe. Since all Arcturian communications to us pass through these personal filters, the information may or may not be coming through 100% accurately. And since we are individuals, we don't all have the same vocabulary, the same knowledge base, or the same life experience. I think that affects how the Arcturians communicate with us. They speak to us in whatever way they need to in order for us to understand them. Each person also chooses what and how much information he or she wants to share with everyone else (in a book, for example). So what we have right now is a kind of patchwork of information, and we're waiting for the rest of the blanks to be filled in.

Some pieces of the picture are extremely clear, however. A huge part of the Reptilian agenda is to create and promote fear, dissent, and negativity among humans. The Arcturians, who represent heaven's enlightened Celestial Command, are here to show us how to defeat that agenda by raising our vibrational frequency and eliminating the negative energy that currently surrounds us. They already vibrate at a much higher frequency than we do. That's one of the reasons they choose to communicate with us the way they do rather than manifesting in the third dimension here on Earth, even though they are capable of doing so. Another reason they don't just show themselves to us is that they follow the universal laws and won't interfere in the karmic paths of others.

---

[8] El Morya is the Ascended Master known as the Chohan of the First (or Blue) Ray. He has incarnated on this planet numerous times, including as Abraham and as Melchior (one of the three wise men). His Ascension took place in 1898, and he now works closely with Archangel Michael to protect humanity from negative influences.

Their energy is powerful, yet very subtle. You have to stop and clear your mind; you have to look and listen for it. You'll know it when you experience it.

Given the age of their civilization, their much higher vibrational frequency, and the fact that most of them have a life span of 350 to 400 Earth years, it isn't surprising the Arcturians have a vastly different and much broader perspective than we have. They see not only the present, but also the past and the future. They have already experienced the transformation we are undergoing now.

Of course, I don't know everything there is to know about the Arcturians. No one human being does. But one thing I am certain of is that they definitely *do* have dominion over the Reptilians. And it is vital for everyone on Earth to become aware of this now.

Their Mission on Earth

The primary focus of the Arcturian civilization is spiritual enlightenment, and their mission is to help others—especially those of us on Earth—to open our hearts and begin the journey to higher consciousness. They want to help us understand God, ourselves, and the nature of the universe. Their communications with us contain not only thoughts but energy patterns. Their technology, along with their energy and thought patterns, can help us heal.

Other advanced civilizations helped the Arcturians in the early stages of their development, and now the Arcturians, in turn, are here to help us with our development. They want nothing more than for us to join them in the Light. They are excellent teachers, and they want us to invite them in. In fact, they have a vested interest in teaching and helping us because doing so generates positive karma for them. They, too, are on a path of learning and evolving to even higher realms.

The Arcturians have been in existence since long before the Earth came to be. They have a special relationship with this planet. Since

Arcturians were the original colonizers and inhabitants of Earth, they have had a connection with the planet and with all of us who inhabit it from the very beginning.

The Arcturians who first came here to colonize Earth left here long ago after their civilization on Earth was destroyed. But they worked closely with other extraterrestrials, such as the Pleiadians[9] and the Andromedans[10], who subsequently seeded the Earth after the Arcturians had left it. Since then, the Arcturians have remained aware of us, and they have been protecting us all along. They have a very high regard for Terra, as they refer to Earth, and feel a sense of responsibility toward us. It is because the Arcturians have been watching over and protecting us that we no longer have more Reptilians coming to the planet.

Their mental powers are so highly developed they can not only move and manifest objects telepathically, but they are also able to travel to other dimensions, both higher and lower. They do so by creating and opening portals. Just by opening a portal to Earth, they are bringing us light and positive energy.

How They Can Help Us

We need that positive energy. The Arcturians say the energy that has been vibrating on this planet makes it difficult for us to remain

---

[9] Peaceful and non-threatening, the Pleiadians are the extraterrestrials who most resemble humans, and many humans have an affinity for them. They are multidimensional beings whose original home was destroyed by the Reptilians. They are now living in the Pleiades star system, where they encountered the Arcturians, who taught them how to protect their new home from the Reptilians. Now the Pleiadians are working with the Arcturians to help rid our planet of Reptilians and to assist us with the process of spiritual transformation.

[10] The Andromedans are humanoid type extraterrestrials from the constellation Andromeda. Like the Arcturians and the Pleiadians, they are high-vibrational beings and members of the Galactic Federation. They, too, work with Christ Consciousness and are here to help this planet. They communicate telepathically and have a high degree of scientific mastery. Lately, the Pleiadians and the Andromedans have been coming through more and more often.

positive and to open our hearts and connect with Source. Although humans are very emotional creatures, we don't really exercise much control over our emotions. It's more like our emotions control us. That's why it's so easy for us to fall into negative states, such as anger, fear, greed, envy, hatred, and despair, which weaken us and make us easy prey for the Reptilians. The Arcturians have learned self-discipline. They know how to balance the positive and the negative, the yin and the yang. They have mastered their emotions, and that mastery has allowed them to make the great spiritual and technological progress they've made.

They point out that we humans tend to let our minds wander. We don't pay enough attention to what we think, what we say, what we feel, and what we do. The Arcturians advise us to not waste our energy or let the negativity around us drain it away. To gain mastery over our thoughts, words, emotions, and deeds, all of which are sources of energy, we must understand how powerful they—and we—actually are.

Humans are also extremely competitive. We compete with each other, and we compete with other ethnic groups, religions, cultures, and countries. Winning is very important to many of us, as is the competition for money and resources. Competition brings out aggression. It implies there's a lack or scarcity of whatever we're competing for. When someone wins, someone else loses. As long as we're occupied pitting ourselves against each other, we can't cooperate to solve our problems. Competition contributes to much of the strife on the planet. The Arcturians say we need to open and develop our heart centers because that's where truth is revealed. Once we're able to see that duality, which we take for granted, is actually an illusion, we'll be able to forsake competition with each other and resonate with a more loving vibration.

Since the Arcturians are a non-dual group consciousness, they don't have the distraction of competition. And their attention isn't focused on personal gain or personal security. That's one of the reasons their civilization is at peace while ours is always at war somewhere on the planet. They have said that all this competition is what ages us and makes us hold onto our fears. And fear feeds right into the Reptilian agenda. The Reptilians want us to face off against each other rather than against them.

Because the Arcturians are not competitive, each being contributes knowledge, talents, and abilities to the whole. They all work together. As a result, the Arcturians are vastly more technologically advanced than we are. Their scientific and technical expertise, along with their ability to act as one consciousness, makes them so much stronger and more powerful than the Reptilians. Although in physical form, they are slender beings only about three to four feet tall, which is much smaller than the Reptilians, they are *of the Light*—and the Light is always stronger than darkness.

As a result of the situation we're in on Earth right now, we aren't capable of dealing with the Reptilians by ourselves. We have a hard time transcending all the negativity they've created. That's why the Arcturians, along with extraterrestrial beings from many other places in the universe, have come to assist us. But it's the Arcturians who have had the longest ongoing relationship with us and who are doing the most to help us, whether we're aware of their help or not.

Like us, they were once three-dimensional beings. They want to see us ascend to the fourth, and then finally to the fifth dimension, as they have done. And they are actively—not passively—assisting us. Because of current conditions, which include the heightened activity of the Reptilians and the very real possibility that we are on a path that could lead to destruction of the planet, the Arcturians are making a greater effort to make themselves known to us now. They are in numerous countries all over the planet. Although they are only working directly with a small fraction of the population, that number is rapidly increasing. I meet more and more people who tell me they are connected to the Arcturians. There are also many Arcturian starseeds—Arcturians who have chosen to incarnate as third-dimensional human beings—who are living among us and helping us.

As beings of the Light, the Arcturians have achieved the high spiritual state known as Christ Consciousness. This state of awareness is sought by people of all religions and cultures, not only Christians. It represents the awakening to our true nature, our connection with Source, with the Divine, with the All—whatever you prefer to call it. To help us achieve Christ Consciousness, the Arcturians work closely with the archangels and with Jesus, also known as Sananda, who is one of the Ascended Masters and a great teacher and healer.

Other extraterrestrials such as the Pleiadians are bringing an emotional message to us. But as the Arcturians have told us, their particular communications with us are primarily mental rather than emotional because they want to help us develop our mental bodies. But this doesn't mean they don't experience love or that they aren't communicating with us out of love. As they have said over and over, their mission is of the heart.

They are using a variety of methods to educate us and make us aware of themselves and of the possibilities that await us. They communicate with me telepathically. They communicate with some people in the dream state, although those people may or may not remember their interactions with the Arcturians when they awaken. I generally don't remember my dreams, but quite a few people I've worked with have detailed recall of their dreams, which I find fascinating. These dreams almost always have something to do with what's going on in the spiritual world, especially if it involves discarnates, demons, or Reptilians. The Arcturians use the dream state when they can't communicate with someone consciously, so sometimes communication in the dream state is a precursor to conscious telepathic communication.

The Arcturians' message of love, peace, and enlightenment may come to us through the medical or healing fields, from the arts, entertainment, or media, or from some other source. Not everyone will understand the message or be open to receiving it, and we still have the freedom of choice to ignore it if that's what we want to do. You can be sure that the Reptilians are doing their utmost to try to block the message and prevent us from "getting" it.

Multidimensional Beings

This universe contains many different dimensions. The Arcturians exist in the fifth dimension, which has a different vibrational frequency. They can also manifest in the third and fourth dimensions, although most of them choose not to do that. They tell us the Ascended Masters exist primarily in the seventh dimension but are able to access all dimensions.

The fourth dimension is without time and space, so those who exist in the fourth dimension know that what my guides have told me is true: that is, everything—past, present, and future—is really all happening at the same time. And that time is now, this very moment.

There is a sense of peace and harmony in the fourth dimension, of going beyond ego boundaries and seeing that we truly are all one.

We already have access to the fourth dimension in the dream state. To begin to access it consciously, we need to open our heart centers. Jesus came to Earth to teach us love and forgiveness, the qualities of the fourth dimension, and to help us open our hearts and raise our vibrational frequency. The Arcturians are here to remind us that is what we need to do if we want to survive and make the leap into higher consciousness.

In the fifth dimension, which the Arcturians say has the quality of "heaven," beings are able to use their thoughts to create or manifest anything their souls desire from a place of love and light. There is a sense of great expansiveness. Communication is telepathic and instantaneous—faster than the speed of light—propelled by the electromagnetic energy of the universe. Beings in the fifth dimension exist within their light bodies, free of the physical demands and limitations of the third dimension.

The fifth-dimensional vibrations from Arcturus affect the rest of the universe and are powerful enough to penetrate all of the beings who are on the same path of love and light.

From our third-dimensional perspective, it's difficult to imagine a dimension without separation and polarity, where the connection to Source is direct and never-ending. But they've told us that, in one sense, we're already there.

The Starship Athena

When I started to research the Arcturians the day after they gave me the download, I was shocked to discover the Arcturian starship now hovering over Earth is named Athena. But that really resonated, too, and it just opened everything up for me. Yes, Athena is the name of a Greek goddess, but that isn't the Athena who is my guide. My guide is Athena, the Arcturian ship, which they refer to as "her." As soon as I found that out, I understood why she has been one of my guides right from the beginning.

It isn't really surprising that one of the Arcturians' ships is named after a Greek goddess. They've told us they visited the Earth during the height of the Greek civilization and interbred with humans at that time. Was the goddess Athena actually an Arcturian? I don't know. She's an Ascended Master, "the ambassador for Cosmic Truth," and is a member of the Karmic Board of the Planetary Hierarchy of the universe. One of her roles is to uphold the ideals of integrity and truth and to give us the will to achieve.

Athena is a well-known figure in Greek mythology, highly esteemed by that civilization. She is considered to be the goddess of wisdom and the goddess of war. But in regard to war, her expertise was in the area of military planning and strategy as opposed to physical fighting. (Ares, the Greek god of war and violence, on the other hand, was *not* held in high esteem by the Greeks.)

The goddess Athena was intelligent, strong, confident, and had a very clear head. She reacted wisely and maturely instead of emotionally. She also had an androgynous aspect, which is how the Arcturians have described themselves to us.

The starship Athena appears to have been built specifically for the Arcturian mission on Earth. Although it is a complex and technically advanced spacecraft, it wasn't designed for battle. It is, however, equipped for protection. Just as the goddess Athena protected her namesake city of Athens, the starship Athena now protects Earth.

The Arcturians gave Norma Milanovich a very detailed description of the starship and its 35 different compartments. Since I've been flying planes since age 16, I found the information about the ship quite interesting. One day when I was inside my house meditating and reading about the Arcturians, I happened to look out the window, and I saw a space ship moving across the sky. It was extremely long, but it didn't make any noise whatsoever. It traveled toward the towers at the crest of the Sandia Mountains and then between them. After just a few seconds, it was gone. There was no question it was an Arcturian ship they wanted me to see. That's the one and only time I've ever seen one of their ships physically instead of in my visions.

I've been on the starship Athena more than once, although I don't remember much about those experiences. The first time I was on one of their ships was a couple of years ago when I was once again meditating. In addition to enormous ships like Athena, the Arcturians have numerous smaller ships that carry only a handful of Arcturians. They took me up in one that had about five Arcturians on it. Not only did they give me a ride in the little ship, they also let me take control of it! On a regular plane, you're strapped in because if the plane tips or rolls and you aren't strapped in, you'll fall out of your seat. No one on the Arcturian ship was strapped in, including me. I put that craft in a spin and everyone inside stayed in an upright position while the ship rotated around us. I'd never imagined anything like that. It was just amazing.

They'd brought me up into the ship so we could travel to the place where a friend of mine worked; she'd told me they were having all kinds of problems over there. The ship travels telepathically, so as soon as you think where you want to go—*boom!*—you're there. Just like that. When we arrived in the vicinity of my friend's workplace, the Arcturians sent down a shaft of light and brought her up into the ship. They continued shining the light, and suddenly I saw two creatures in Reptilian form trying to flee. I said, "Get 'em!" One of the two got outside the shaft of light, and the Arcturians grabbed it. Both of them went fast—straight up into the Light!

My friend called me the next day and said, "You won't believe this weird dream I had." In her dream, she essentially saw what I just described. I had to tell her we'd been up in the ship together because she had no recollection of it. We weren't in the ship physically, obviously, but in an etheric state.

Now I can go up in one of those little ships anytime I want to, but I don't do it very often. The starship Athena has a healing chamber, and once you're connected with the Arcturians, I think you can go there whenever you feel you need a healing. Sometimes before I go to sleep, I'll ask them to take me up and put me through the healing room and fill me with their blue light. Since I don't remember my dreams, I generally don't remember those trips.

I've also visited the planet Arcturus. In early 2011, I was attending a conference and got into a conversation with two women who had been connecting with the Arcturians for a long time. They told me we could go to Arcturus anytime. We went around a corner to a private area where we all got into a meditative state, and they said, "Let's go up to the ship Athena." So we went to the ship and from there to Arcturus. This happened instantaneously; there was no time delay. The women asked me what I was seeing on planet Arcturus, and I told them I saw a male figure sitting on a beach looking at a huge lake. The lake wasn't water, though, it was liquid light. And inside the lake of liquid light, way down below, was a huge crystal. I don't know exactly how big it was, maybe a quarter-mile around, but it was a very powerful healing-type crystal.

The women told me to enter the body of the man on the beach, so I did that, and the next thing I knew, the body got up and entered the lake of liquid light and floated down near the crystal. I remember getting some healing energy down there; I could feel it. Soon I was out of the lake, and then the three of us were back on the ship. None of this took very long. Almost immediately after that, we were back at the conference.

Learning As We Go

When it comes to the Arcturians and the higher dimensions of reality, much of what we learn raises more questions than it answers. And the questions keep multiplying. Eventually some of them get answered, but when will all the questions finally be answered? I don't know. As I've been saying all along, I'm still playing catch-up, and I don't expect that to change.

The most important thing to remember is that the Arcturians are here to help us. They are doing that in many ways: by showing us how to raise our vibrational frequency, by giving us direct healing, and by ridding us of Reptilians.

They will assist anyone who wants to advance spiritually. But if you want their help, you have to ask for it. Unlike the Reptilians who do not honor universal laws, including that of free will, the Arcturians will not interfere without our permission. They are in contact with some of us in the dream state, but they say it is better for us to ask directly to be connected with them.

And that's all we have to do: ask.

Chapter 7
Dropping Seeds?

Seeing Signs of Improvement

After our last session with Carl, I had felt that Saturday would be the day to remove the other two Reptilians, but during the week, I kept having the sense that I didn't need to wait. It could be done at any time. I asked the Arcturians if Carl needed to be present. The answer was, "No." Did I need to tell Carl what I was doing? "No."

Then at 8:07 on Friday evening, I was sitting on the couch reading a book on psychic protection, when the Arcturians came through.

I asked, "All right, go now?" They answered, "Yes."

So I went into a meditative state, and the next thing I knew, the Arcturians were taking the two Reptilians out of Carl. They let me watch as they removed them and took them wherever they take Reptilians. At that point, I didn't know where that was. The visual image I got was a fuzzy, hazy impression, but I don't even get to see that much when a demon or a discarnate is being removed. And I didn't feel the nausea I normally feel when I'm working with demons.

Afterward, I didn't say anything to anyone about it, but the next day Lisa asked me if something had happened around 8:00 the night before. At approximately the same time the Arcturians were working through me to remove the Reptilians from Carl, Lisa had suddenly felt completely drained of energy, and she had an overpowering need to lie down and meditate. She wondered what the significance of that time was. I didn't give her any details about it because I wanted to get confirmation from someone else that the two Reptilians had been removed.

When Carl arrived for his next session with us, Lisa, Robert, and I were in the midst of discussing some of the fascinating experiences we'd been having with the Arcturians. The minute Carl entered the room, Robert said, "Oh, my goodness!" Carl looked much healthier than any of us had ever seen him.

Low key as always, Carl acknowledged he had been doing "pretty well." He gave some credit to the temperate weather and to the various supplements he'd been taking for his skin inflammation. Although he wasn't feeling great all the time, over the past four weeks he'd gradually been feeling better and better, both physically and emotionally. All of us, including Carl, were excited to see any degree of improvement in his condition and his sense of well-being, and this improvement was very noticeable.

I reminded him that the work we were doing wouldn't be concluded overnight and that the healing team still wasn't making any guarantees in terms of an outcome. Carl was hoping we could give him some kind of a time frame but said he understood we couldn't be more specific or accurate at that point. We reviewed what had happened so far, beginning with my first individual session with him, during which we removed two demons and two discarnates.

The story we had originally gotten from the three Reptilians—that Carl contained within himself critical information from them that he was required to access and put into writing in order to heal—had changed abruptly once we caught onto their actual agenda. Now we were trying to help Carl exercise his free will and reclaim his body, which is what he'd wanted all along.

His understanding of the situation was that "there's something in there that's foreign to me . . . and I'm hoping it's true and it can be removed, if it hasn't already been, because that would make my life a lot easier."

When Carl mentioned that he *hoped* it was true, I asked both Robert and Lisa if either one had any doubt whatsoever that it was true. Both said "no" quite emphatically. Robert acknowledged that a certain amount of trust was involved in the process we were going through, as well as a testing of our faith, yet he was certain the work was worthwhile. He believed we were doing the right thing in the right way. Lisa said she had wanted to doubt herself, but her conviction about what we were doing was too strong. I did not have an iota of doubt, either.

The spiritual and metaphysical experiences Carl had had over the past 20 years led him to believe "it's there"—meaning, among other things, that the entities were real. That's why he kept coming back and meeting with us. Although he had a lot of personal doubt, he didn't doubt the possibility that the entities we'd been engaging could be the source of his severe health problems.

Having reaffirmed our belief in this process, we said a prayer for protection and asked to connect with our guides.

Leaving Seeds Behind

I then told everyone about the removal of the other two Reptilians that had taken place since the last session. Lisa confirmed that the two Reptilians had indeed been removed, but they had left behind what looked to her like little seeds. They hadn't all left seeds. The first one who had been taken went so quickly he didn't have a chance. But one of the smaller ones who'd just been removed had left three seeds. The message Lisa heard from the Arcturians was that the energy work being done with Carl needed to continue in order to prevent those seedlings from sprouting.

We were all new at dealing with these things, and we didn't yet know what they really were. Carl wondered if they could be "seed buds for more Reptilians to grow out of." Lisa thought the seeds, which she saw as being in the right shoulder area of Carl's body, functioned as a beacon or a tracking device. "They can't be nurtured," she said. "Don't water them or allow them to grow or mature, because the Reptilians are just going to start building themselves right back up." She was certainly right about that. But we didn't know then that we could ask the Arcturians to remove them, just as they had removed the three Reptilians.

Carl had no awareness of the seeds being inside him. He said he was so used to having something in him all the time that he didn't know what it would feel like not to have anything.

A tremendous amount of healing had been done on Carl, but he was not yet entirely free. There was still a link between him and some-place outside of him that needed to be severed and completely sealed off. Otherwise, the Reptilians would be able to harass and control him at will. He might feel better for a short time, but then he would start feeling bad again, and the cycle would continue.

The Arcturians had been telling us all along that we needed to make sure Carl got a lot of healing during this process, and that message came through loud and clear. Lisa was experiencing pain on her right side, and she saw a vortex in the corner of the room that was pulling at her. Robert felt a "tug" in the area of his solar plexus, an area where Carl also had a lot of physical discomfort. We needed to do a healing, not just for Carl, but for all of us.

Lisa said we had to do it immediately. I agreed.

I called in the Arcturians, and also Orion, who had promised us protection, and I asked for a special cleanse. On behalf of all of us in the room, I asked that, if possible, the negative energy associated with Carl—the seeds, connection, cord, portal, vortex, whatever it was—end now. Right away I felt a huge release. Robert said he felt very warm. And Lisa described seeing a shaft of light coming from above and going straight down into the seedlings, "just a beautiful white light."

I thanked everyone—Arcturians, Orion, the rest of our guides—who had been present and assisting us with Carl, since the three of us weren't entirely sure what we were doing. How could we be? We were simply showing up and doing what we were asked to do.

As soon as I called on Orion, Robert sensed a wave of energy rush forward and through me. *Whoosh!* Everyone felt a big shift in the energy.

Lisa visualized the white light turning into a vortex of light that continued to expand as it shone down on the seedlings. "In this forest, which is a metaphor for Carl's body," she said, "all the trees started catching on fire."

Carl was receiving a major cleanse from the inside out. Lisa saw that the seeds were now "charcoal," but the Arcturians were still working. We asked them to get rid of all the particles, every last one, so nothing could reattach, and to clean each of us from inside and out, as well as clean the entire house and the area around the house. I mentioned each of us by name and went remotely to everyone else's house, too, including Carl's. Cleanse, cleanse, cleanse—cleanse the houses and all the people who lived in them. I had been learning just how specific I needed to be when I asked for something, rather than making the assumption the Arcturians would follow my unspoken intent. And I had to allow enough time instead of rushing through the cleansing process. Cleanse every-thing. Cleanse it completely!

We all felt much lighter afterward. Robert had more flexibility in his neck. And I was affected so deeply I couldn't even continue talking.

Carl said he'd felt quite a bit—for him. He felt a *whoosh* first, and then he saw the light. "I don't normally see light going through me like this, but it was coming up through me this time. I felt a shift. There's no question about it."

That was encouraging to the rest of us and gave Carl a sense of comfort that at least something *somewhere* was shifting.

Inviting the Light In

Carl was still longing for clarity. "Just anything that I can know for sure. Just clarity about something. What the hell am I here for?" He laughed, but we all knew exactly how serious he was.

Robert told Carl the Arcturians wanted him to be aware how unusual his experiences were. Since there were other people in similar situations, if Carl eventually chose to talk or write about his experiences, others could draw considerable strength from him.

But he wasn't there yet. I sensed that the information deep within him would be released a little bit at a time, like a time-release capsule. As he got better, he'd know where he needed to go. Right now, though, he just needed to be gentle with himself and try to reconnect with who he really is. If he just let it happen, everything else would fall into place.

Robert encouraged Carl to imagine opening the windows of a dusty mansion and allowing sunlight to penetrate. "Invite the light from the sun into you."

Carl said he had actually been standing outside in the sun every day for the past few weeks, which was something he hadn't been able to do until recently. Before now, he hadn't been able to tolerate the sun on his face because of the condition of his skin. "But I've always craved the sun and the light," he said.

He mentioned again that when he had first started searching for answers 18 years ago, he thought he was on the right path, but then "I got shut down."

Robert wasn't surprised. He told Carl that as the light comes in, it exposes anything that isn't in harmony with it. When Carl started opening himself up to the energy and the light so many years ago, a spotlight shone down on all those entities. Everything dark inside him rejected that light and screamed out against it. "Whoa! No way! This is not going to happen." His body then turned into the battleground it was when he first came to see me.

But why was his suffering so intense and prolonged? Robert said he was healing a number of things, not just from this lifetime but from previous lifetimes as well. Lisa was able to see some of his past lives, and she asked him if he wanted to hear about it. Of course, he did.

"It looks like you had some darkness in past lifetimes," she said. "You were wearing some kind of papal hat, like a priest's or a pope's, and you gave the order to execute many people." In that life, which took place before the Inquisition, Carl was very angry and cruel. Lisa saw many people around him crying and begging for mercy as Carl turned his back and strode into a palace or a church. She sensed these activities had continued over several years, during which he caused a great deal of suffering for others and deprived people of their freedom. Many people came to him for sympathy or compassion, but he didn't have any.

Carl had heard some of this before from another psychic a long time ago, so it jibed with what he already knew. He also believed he had been a warrior during several lifetimes. In a later lifetime, he had been an advanced healer and was burned at the stake for refusing to heal a tribal leader. Afterward, he said, he brought that anger and rage into his next incarnation, to try to heal it.

"I've been burning for it a long time this time," he said.

We knew that after the removal of the three Reptilians and the cleanse we'd just completed we would need at least two sessions of flushing Carl out with light energy. Lisa thought we could work on him individually, but we ultimately agreed this wasn't the time to separate.

We needed to continue the joint effort and do it together. Clearly, there was power in our numbers.

Chapter 8
Two Steps Forward, One Step Back

"Can I Get Re-infected?"

Unfortunately, the next time we met, Carl wasn't doing nearly as well. He had a dental appointment scheduled for the next day and needed $4,000 worth of work done. That was in addition to approximately $10,000 he'd spent on his teeth the year before. He'd already had several teeth pulled, and along with getting a bridge, he might need to have another tooth pulled. He told us his teeth had gotten weak as a result of his illness, and they had become very vulnerable to cavities especially in the past few years. But finding out he might need to get another tooth pulled was still a shock for him.

"I hate having to go back there," he said. "It's just traumatic."

The Arcturians told me Carl's dental problems were not related to the Reptilians; Lisa sensed they were the result of his inner anger.

But Carl's most immediate concern was the possibility of getting "re-infected." He acknowledged he wasn't very good at protecting himself or being able to tell when anything, such as a discarnate, might be coming at him.

I felt that he *was* being protected to a certain extent because my guides told me he was. But Carl still needed to learn how to be "a good housekeeper and gate guardian," as Robert put it; otherwise, he could end up back in trouble again. Robert suggested Carl start taking time to cleanse his house whenever he went out. Carl said he had tried smudging, and although that bothered his allergies, he knew there were other things he could do to lighten and shift the energy. Robert also wanted Carl to start protecting himself with light whenever he left his house. He could ask the angels and archangels to protect him and visualize himself covered in light. Lastly, Carl should try to remember to cleanse again before re-entering his house and after anyone else visited him.

Lisa described how she creates a sun orb around herself when she goes out in public. "I just have the sun come from my heart chakra outward, like an egg-shaped orb of golden light, so nothing can penetrate it."

Although he had trouble remembering to do those kinds of things, Carl he said he would make an effort.

I told him to use whatever worked for him when he left his house and when he returned. His energy and vibrational frequency were still low enough that he wasn't able to completely fend for himself, so the angels and archangels and the Arcturians were watching over him. Because he was in such a vulnerable state, he was under their special protection. They were with him at all times, surrounding him. But he still needed to learn to be more mindful and aware of what was going on around him and to practice techniques to protect himself. (You can find out more about how to protect yourself in Chapter 12.)

In the meantime, because of that special protection, I didn't believe Carl was going to, in his words, "get slammed again." If he did, he knew where to turn for help.

He said he hoped that one day he would be as certain about all of this as the rest of us were. But doubt was the norm for him after so many years of illness and frustration. He'd had little experience of being effective in making positive changes. The process he was going through might be two steps forward and one step back, but to me that was a lot better than remaining stagnant, or even worse, continually sliding backwards.

Telling Jose's Story

Before we began working on Carl, however, Lisa and I had something to share with him and with Robert. Over the weekend, we did a healing on Jose, the boyfriend of a woman we had previously worked with. The woman thought she had seen three demons on top of Jose's head, and she tried to engage them. That didn't go very well so she got him to make an appointment with me. When someone has demons, I usually get nauseous just talking to that person on the telephone. But in this case, I didn't. Nor did I feel nauseous when Jose arrived for his appointment.

When we all sat down together for the healing, the very same thing happened that had happened with Carl and a few others: Jesus, Michael, and the rest all just stood there. I asked Jose if he was not allowing Jesus in. I wasn't feeling anything, though, so I was pretty sure we were dealing with Reptilians, and they were blocking me. I looked over at Lisa to get some confirmation. Her eyes were closed, but after a few seconds she opened them and looked at me. She said she saw three hooded figures, the one in the middle larger than the other two. And they had started attacking her neck, just as they had when we were working with Carl. I told Lisa to disengage immediately.

I asked Orion and the Arcturians if they could take care of the Reptilians, and they said, "Yes." Lisa asked the same question and also got an affirmative response.

Then they started to take all three of them. I said, "Are you sure? You want to do all of them?" They did. They took the three of them at once, right then and there. It was amazing.

Once the Reptilians were gone, one demon was finally able to leave. And then another one left. After that, five discarnate spirits were taken to the Light, too. Jose had served in the military during the Gulf War, and the discarnates were Persians.

"While he was over there," Lisa said, "they ran right into him. He was like an open portal."

Without a doubt, it was the most powerful healing session I'd been involved in up to that point. Carl's had also been very powerful, but in Jose's case, we were able to remove the three Reptilians together, and then multiple demons and discarnates, all in the same session.

We then closed the portal that connected Jose with the Reptilians. Lisa believes the Reptilians are capable of "dimension-hopping." They enter and leave our dimension through these portals. The Reptilians we removed from Jose had entered him when he was around three years of age, which was a different situation from Carl's since he had been born with them.

When Lisa spoke with Jose afterward, he told her he felt like he'd had surgery. He was in bed for a couple of days, and he just kept purifying and cleansing. He said he'd lost 14 pounds in three days! I was shocked. How was his body able to handle that? Of course, he was physically stronger than Carl and about 20 years younger, so that probably made a difference in how he responded to the healing.

But we wouldn't have known what to do with Jose had we not done this first with Carl. It was a steep learning curve for all of us.

Guided or Misguided?

Carl was understandably frustrated that he hadn't had as positive a response as Jose's. He wasn't aware of any changes in his thinking, but I thought it might be too soon for him to have that kind of clarity after having had Reptilians inside him all his life. He didn't really know his own mind yet.

We needed to make sure we were closing everything off in Carl and not leaving any open portals for the Reptilians to use. We also wanted to give him as much help and as much healing as we could to shift his frequency and raise his vibration, which was difficult for him to do for himself after his lifetime of conditioning.

Carl had been trained in Reiki[11], and although he hadn't practiced it in a very long time, he used to be able to bring through the light and the Reiki energy. Robert thought it would help him if he started doing that again, but Carl was concerned about "bringing in more energy." He'd been told several times he had "too much energy" coming in, and it was backing up and contributing to his illness. I wasn't sure what he meant by that, and I don't think he really was, either.

Over the years—decades, even—Carl had been to so many different types of practitioners, healers, and psychics that all of us, including him, had a difficult time sorting everything out. He was overloaded with information about what was going on with him, and some of the work he'd done appears to have been at cross-purposes. He had also had at least a couple of major setbacks as a result of following the suggestions of one or another practitioner. As a result, he was confused and afraid to try anything that might make him feel worse. And Reiki, he said, did not necessarily make him feel good.

This is one of the reasons I generally discourage people from seeking or receiving any other type of treatment during the first three to six weeks they're working with me. When you see one person and then another person and yet another person, each of whom has a different perspective and a different approach, all it does is complicate the situation. If you've seen a variety of people and tried all kinds of

---

[11] Reiki is a Japanese method of healing, relaxation, and stress-reduction. It involves the "laying on of hands" (although not all practitioners physically touch the subject) in order to access and increase one's life-force energy.

techniques and treatments and are still not feeling any better, you can begin to doubt you'll *ever* get better. Eventually that doubt and fear can expand to the point where you convince yourself there's nothing that can help you. The worst part about it is you're then unable to help yourself.

Channeling had also been suggested to Carl as a way to move the supposed excess energy through him. Although he'd made a couple of attempts, he hadn't been able to stick with it and admitted he wasn't really open to it.

"I never was relaxed enough to let it just come through me," he said. "Not even 20 years ago. I've been skeptical for a long time, and pissed off, so I'm just not open to it."

But Carl wouldn't have been able to channel when he'd had those Reptilians in him. And even if he had been able to do it, what would he have been channeling? I always advise people who want to learn how to channel to have any entities removed beforehand. Demons and Reptilians will block people and impede their connection with Source. Once those entities are removed, most people have no problem connecting.

It was just as well Carl hadn't been able to channel when he'd tried it before, but his lack of success increased his doubt about being able do anything positive or effective on his own behalf.

He thought his left brain was getting in the way of his being able to engage his right brain, which was probably true. He knew meditating was one way to engage his right brain, but meditation was also hard for him. That was no surprise to me, either. How can you quiet your mind to meditate with all those entities—especially Reptilians—chattering away inside it? You can't.

Now that the Reptilians were gone, channeling, meditating, and even Reiki were legitimate options and tools he could use to help him raise his vibration. But knowing what to do and doing it are two different things.

More Work to Do

What else could *we* do for him, as a group? Robert asked the Arcturians if all the portals in Carl were closed. The answer was "no." Robert then had a vision of between three and five portals inside Carl's spine. The Arcturians told Robert the portals were at the DNA level, which meant they had been in Carl's body from the beginning. If he still had these portals, why hadn't he had any more Reptilian visitors? We thought it might be due to the extra protection he was receiving at the moment; we didn't yet know that once Reptilians have been removed from someone, that person cannot get them ever again.

The Arcturians asked us to direct light at Carl's spine. If we actually ran light down his spine, we could secure and heal the portals. So I asked Robert and Lisa to fill Carl with light and to visualize the light going through his spine. I stood behind Carl with my hands on his shoulders. As soon as we got started, I felt a powerful electrical jolt, and Carl said he could feel the heat from my hands.

Lisa saw the Arcturians sending light up and down Carl's spine and also to the area around his jaw. After a short time, she saw that the top three portals had been closed, but the two lower ones were still open.

Robert noticed that all the energy had been concentrated around the top of Carl's shoulders. He felt we were trying to get down near Carl's tailbone, but we hadn't quite been able to do it. So I asked that we all focus on the lower area of Carl's spine. As we did that, both Lisa and Robert sensed that the portals were in between the chakras.

"And they're very dense in their magnetism," Lisa said. "Very dense."

We succeeded in pushing the light through the fourth portal. The fifth one was especially resistant, so I told everyone to get ready for a big push and that finally did it—we got the light through that one, too. Lisa suggested we finish by showering light over Carl's entire body.

I felt we could all benefit from a shower of light.

Robert saw that all the portals in Carl's spine had been healed. "I saw all of the chakra colors being illuminated and balanced," he said. "I then saw his aura being filled with white light, and a beautiful gold light being put around it to protect him. It feels strong and clear at the moment."

Taking One Step at a Time

I was glad we had been able to accomplish this task, but why had it even come up now? What else needed to be done that we weren't yet aware of? Were we not asking the Arcturians in the right way? Was our energy not strong enough? Was it that Carl could only handle a little bit at a time? I was getting impatient. I wanted it done. All of it.

Robert reminded us we had been told the work on Carl would have to be done in stages, which is why he'd been so surprised when Lisa and I told him how many entities we'd removed from Jose over the weekend. But again, Jose was younger and stronger and had not had the Reptilian bloodline.

"That's why we're seeing it in your spine," Robert told Carl. "It's in your body, and it's almost like ripping someone's spine out. It's right down at the genetic code level. So we've got to go a stage at a time."

That reminded me of our first group session when Carl's mother had come through and told us the possession Carl was dealing with went back three generations. She had mentioned his DNA, and Lisa, too, had picked up on the fact that Carl had something in his bloodline. We just hadn't had enough information to put the pieces together. This also explained why other healers who had seen the Reptilians saw them as feelers or transmitters instead of entities—because they were part of Carl's body, entwined in his DNA.

I asked if there was anything else, anything more, that we could do at this time, and the answer was "no." Robert didn't think there were any more portals to close or entities to remove, but the work was not yet done. Using the house metaphor again, we had finished gutting the house and now it was time to remodel.

"The person who's in charge of the house has never had a chance to wander around and look at it," Robert said. He told Carl that in order to prevent problems from creeping back in, he needed to learn to look after the house, which he had never had to—or been able to—do before now. Robert also acknowledged Carl's anger about all he'd had to go through.

"I'm just hoping it's going to stop," Carl said. "That it's going to start to heal."

Robert reminded him about getting into the habit of protecting and cleansing on a regular basis. If necessary, we would help him find something that worked for him to bring the light in and get him any assistance he needed to do it. But he was still resistant to the idea he could help himself.

"I tried to do those kinds of things before," he said, "and look what's happened."

Robert contended the situation was quite different now. But as we'd seen, the result of Carl's experiences had destroyed his faith in himself and his own abilities. That may have been the biggest obstacle he was facing now. And there was only so much we could do to help him over it. Robert thought it might be beneficial for him to join a group of people who channeled or did some type of light work to make it easier on himself.

Carl had been stagnant for such a long time and had seen no improvement in his health and well-being. But recently he had been moving forward. It may have been two steps forward and one step back, but that's progress. Slow, steady progress. No one could predict how long the entire recovery process would take, but whether he could see or acknowledge it or not, I could see that he was making progress.

"Baby steps," Lisa said. "They're showing me you have to take baby steps."

Because his physical difficulties were making it so hard for him to take action on his own behalf, I referred him to another psychic. She was also a medical intuitive, which was not an ability anyone in our group had at that time. Carl was reluctant, but he agreed to see her, at least for one session.

Just then, I felt the presence of Carl's mother among us. Lisa also sensed her presence and conveyed her words of encouragement to her son. She told Carl he had had something toxic in his body that had nothing to do with the Reptilians, but he had the power to push that toxicity out. She said his healing would come from within. She was with him always, and she had pulled all of us together to work with him. She urged him to connect with his higher self. His guides were available for him to call upon, as were the Arcturians, to help with his healing.

Carl's mother also told him to call upon the Andromedans to fill him with a creative vibration. She wanted him to paint, to create some kind of visual art to help open a softer part of himself. Lisa saw the color pink associated with that opening.

"I am sending you much love and light, my dear son."

Carl acknowledged he had to be willing to try it one more time, even though he was skeptical and lacked faith in himself. Even if he didn't believe anything he did would work.

His doubt was in himself, not in anything the healing team had said or done. "I've been aware of this from things I've seen and experienced many times over. But that doesn't change the fact that I haven't been able to do anything about it."

I told him he wouldn't have results overnight, but the opportunity was there for a new beginning, a new lease on life. He now had a chance to reprogram himself. Best of all, he had a choice. He hadn't had a choice before.

"It feels frightening," Carl said. "Like I've been cut loose."

We all assured him we were not cutting him loose. In fact we agreed to meet again in two weeks. That would give him an opportunity to practice cleansing and protecting himself and his house and becoming more aware of what was going on around him.

Robert told him he was a very brave soul. With all he'd gone through, it was amazing to the rest of us that Carl was still alive.

"Oh, yes," Carl said. "Still alive. That I can agree with."

Chapter 9
Peeling the Onion

Healing Old Karma

In the intervening two weeks, which included the Thanksgiving holiday, Carl seemed to have "picked something up," as we refer to it. Robert, Lisa, and I all felt him before he arrived, and whatever he had was already engaging Robert and me. We were both extremely nauseated, which usually indicates a demonic presence. So we barely settled into our seats before reciting a prayer for protection and calling in our guides.

Whatever Carl had, there seemed to be more than one. Archangel Michael was able to remove them and send them to the Light, so they weren't Reptilians. Lisa saw an image of something around Carl's throat: "First snakes, and then they turned into a noose."

Carl had been to see Margaret, the medical intuitive I'd referred him to, several times since our last session, and he told us she had seen some kind of an "alien-like creature" clamped around his head. Lisa said it could have been the same thing she'd just seen around his neck. She sensed it had taken a great deal of effort on the part of our guides to pull it—or them—out of him.

But Carl was supposed to have been under special protection. So how had they gotten in?

Margaret had seen a hole in Carl's aura where something had been removed. The hole was now healing, but as Robert said, it could open up again. Another psychic who had been at Margaret's office when Carl was there saw a "sucking kind of creature" at the base of his skull. And when Margaret went over to Carl's house to do a thorough cleanse, she told him he was being attacked in his sleep.

It seemed he was being bombarded. A battle was being waged, and he was the battleground. But why? Robert suggested that the demons and the Reptilians didn't want to give up what they'd lost. Margaret had told Carl he'd gone over to the dark side a number of times in previous lives, and she thought he was on the fence in this one. The battle lines had been drawn between the darkness and the Light.

Then Archangel Michael removed something else from Carl, pulling it up and out of him. Carl said it felt like a rope being drawn up from the middle of his belly. Lisa saw lots of fire in his belly—and lots of anger. "Eyes of red fire." She told him that after she had seen his eyes in an earlier session, they had made such a strong an impression on her that it had taken a couple of days for her to get rid of the sense of rage they'd left her with. Margaret, too, had seen Carl's anger—which he had already acknowledged several times. After suffering physically for more than 15 years, he was extremely angry. Angry and frustrated.

His weak auric shield was allowing these things to get in, but there was some good news along with the bad. Jesus and the archangels now had dominion over him.

Carl believed he'd picked up whatever he'd gotten right after his last session with us, possibly later that night. He'd actually begun feeling bad a day or two earlier. These entities may have already been bothering him when we last saw him, but I hadn't felt them in his energy field then. And it's highly unusual for someone to pick something up that quickly after a healing session, so we were all a bit confused about what was going on.

Archangel Michael took yet another one out of him. As soon as the three of us focused on sending him light, another one went, and then one more. We continued filling Carl with light, while Lisa tried to see what these things were. She thought they were related to his karma, to the lifetimes in which he had held positions of power and had used it for destructive purposes. She saw many people being hanged, burned, and otherwise injured from his abuses of power. Margaret had told Carl that because of the things he'd done in the past, he'd given up his power before coming into this lifetime.

"I remember when I was about 19, I had thoughts that I didn't understand," Carl said. "I felt that I had to be careful not to do what I'd done before. A feeling that I had power and that I had to be very careful not to become a Hitler or something like that. But I didn't understand where those thoughts were coming from. I thought maybe it was something any teenager would come up with."

When the rest of us told him we hadn't had any thoughts like that when we were 19, Carl said he guessed he had been remembering something from his past lives.

The Arcturians had come to Lisa when she was on her way to our session to tell her we would need to call on their crystal light. So we continued sending lots and lots of light to Carl, and after a while his auric shield began to feel better, more intact, and he seemed more relaxed. The process Carl was going through, which we were going through with him, was akin to peeling the layers of an onion. Now that all the other entities had been removed, he had an opportunity to heal a considerable amount of his karma. He might even get to a point where he could do some work on this lifetime.

Margaret had told Carl he'd been taking things on from other people and carrying them in his third chakra. So when Robert balanced Carl's chakras, he concentrated on the third, which was in need of reinforcement. The focus of that chakra is the mental body and will power—and Carl's will power definitely needed strengthening. After Robert finished, Carl said he felt quite a bit calmer.

I still wanted to know why the protection hadn't worked for him after we'd been told he would be protected because of the vulnerable state he was in. What had happened? As we tried to figure it out, we finally realized that nothing had failed to work or gone wrong. *Nothing new had come in*, so he had been protected. All of what we were dealing with now was karmic. It had been there all along, buried beneath several of those onion layers.

Even before Carl arrived for this session, I had told the others I thought we would be working with past-life issues. Karma plays a role in our lives, and none of the guides will interfere with someone's karma because, if they did, it would have a negative impact on their own karma. That's a universal law of cause and effect. And when karmic issues are involved, you can't always resolve everything in one healing (and maybe not even in one lifetime). But now that Carl had nothing new coming in that he was forced to deal with, these older pre-existing issues were being allowed to come to the surface to be healed.

Carl said that immediately after the last balancing Margaret did for him, which occurred two nights ago, he began feeling extremely ill. She tried to do more cleansing to help him, but nothing seemed to work. He continued to feel awful. "Just about everything, my back, my gut, everything was going crazy on me."

That made sense. What Carl was going through now had nothing to do with the Reptilians or any other entities. This was pure Carl, at the soul level. With all the entities gone and so much light and energy being pumped into him, his soul was seizing this new opportunity to heal and release the older issues. And those issues were coming up fast, incredibly fast. The Reptilians never would have allowed it to happen while they were in control.

Arcturians Speak to Carl

As this realization gradually dawned on us, the energy in the room became very high, and I sensed the Arcturians wanted to communicate with us. Robert agreed to channel them. I asked the Arcturians if we were on the right path with Carl. They said that we were. I also wanted to know if Carl would begin experiencing any relief in the near future—relief from his physical symptoms, specifically, but also emotional and spiritual relief, which were equally important.

The Arcturians told us that, as we'd surmised, "energies are now coming forth which could not be cleared before," and they were assisting us in clearing them:

> *It is entirely Carl's decision and choice as to how much he chooses to cleanse at this time. He is making the most of the opportunity, for he understands that he is able to sustain this level of cleansing.*

They were aware all four of us were expecting better health for Carl as a result of the work we were doing with him. But there was a caveat.

> *It is not that the health should be denied, but there is an opportunity for cleansing and healing here, which is what Carl has elected to do. It is, if you wish, a fast track.*

They reiterated that balancing the cleansing and healing with physical improvement was up to Carl. Lisa asked if they could provide some assistance in the way of physical comfort during this period of cleansing and purification. The Arcturians said they were already doing that; however, the person who was "driving" the process was Carl. It was his choice as to how much physical discomfort he wanted to endure. He could always request a "reduction in the speed with which the energies are clearing," and if he did so, he would have a period of respite. The Arcturians recommended three to five days of rest, during which they and any other healing forces Carl called upon would repair and restock his energy levels.

Carl wasn't sure exactly what he needed to do to slow the process down. The Arcturians told him he simply needed to ask. They suggested he do it aloud, which would give him more confidence that what he was asking for would happen. They even gave him the words to use:

Please slow down this process or suspend it for the moment. In its place, please bring through healing light and love energy now.

They told Carl that as soon as he asked for it, they would provide it.

He wanted to know if he would feel better if he slowed things down a great deal. The simple answer was "yes." But the full answer was more complicated, and the situation did not appear to be as straightforward as it had originally sounded. The Arcturians told Carl to remember that his soul was also driving the process.

You have your personality in the third dimension—the small you—and you have the large you at the higher dimensions which can see the greater picture. It is exploiting the opportunity that you have before you, for this window of opportunity does not last forever. Those who offer their light and service [to you] cannot continue to do this for the years to come, and the soul knows this. It is making the most of the moment.

Carl indicated he understood.

Lisa asked the Arcturians if any portals in Carl were still open. They said no, but because he was bringing up new energies into his body for cleansing and release, links or connections to other energies had to be properly healed. If not, they would leave space that could be filled by energies of a similar (lower) frequency. That seems to be what had occurred as a result of Carl's recent work with Margaret.

The Arcturians also told Carl there were no more open portals in his house. An excellent job of cleansing and protecting had been done there. All the portals were closed and no more should open unless Carl invited them in or otherwise elected to have them there.

Lisa wanted to know if Carl could heal his "past life crimes" just by acknowledging them. Was that enough? The Arcturians answered that those actions Carl had taken were choices, and all choices—however we judge them either now or at the time they were made—gain experience. We shouldn't think of them as bad experiences, but simply as experiences, which were "energy in action" and which, therefore, had consequences.

> *What he is now doing is bringing all of those unfinished pieces of energy to a point of conclusion and culmination, and this is done through healing.*

They weren't sure we understood completely, and neither were we, so they tried to make themselves clearer to Carl.

> *At the moment, you perceive yourself as Carl in this lifetime. From a multidimensional perspective, you are many different personalities, and you have lived many different lifetimes, and endured in some cases some very challenging experiences. You were unable to, at that time, complete all of the energy work required. Because the frequency in which you now exist is higher, you are asking that all of those loose ends be brought together and tied up. This is a point of opportunity to heal and cleanse.*

I asked the Arcturians to confirm that Carl—or at least Carl's soul—wanted to be on this fast track, and they said he did. Were Robert, Lisa, and I to continue working with him until he was able to release us and move forward on his own? They said that was a choice for each one of us to make individually.

Carl was still trying to get someone to give him a timeframe. The Arcturians told him that the next three to four months would be the best time to take advantage of the opportunity being presented to him, although the work wouldn't necessarily take that long. Would he be healthier and feel better physically at the end of that time? Again, that depended on the amount of work he did and the balance he chose between processing and resting.

Carl said he hoped he could deal with his fear of suffering and of the unknown.

"Surround Yourself With Love and Light"

The Arcturians encouraged Carl to request the highest frequency of love whenever he received healings, "that which gives the wisdom to know that there is no duality, that in essence fear is the absence of love. Surround yourself with love and light at every opportunity. This will sustain and protect you." They told him they were bringing through that frequency right now and as a result he might feel a little lightheaded or lighter. "Sustain your energy at a higher frequency. This is your greatest protection against fear."

Although Carl was concerned about his ability to bring that frequency through, the Arcturians told him he could do it.

We would tell you that you are powerful. In many incarnations you have been an exceptionally powerful individual and have used energy and power—not always in the way you might choose were you in a similar situation. But you do have the capacity to bring through much, much power. It is available to you because you are reconnecting yourself with each of your previous and future lives. You are remembering that you are a multidimensional being, outside the constraints of time and space.

You have that power at your fingertips, should you choose. . . .
You are much more powerful than you can possibly conceive at
this time. This is why you are seen as so valuable.

So was Carl the only thing holding Carl back now? The Arcturians suggested it was actually Carl's ego that was holding him back.

The personality or ego that is referred to as Carl has some
growth to do. It is always difficult for the ego because it does not
like change. Carl's soul has changed the status quo, and the ego
is feeling very uncomfortable with this . . . . This will be an explo-
ration for you, through your heart center, with your soul. There
are opportunities coming for you very soon, where you would be
able to open up to much, much more light through channeling or
healing.

They also described a simple relaxation process he could use at any time to help him get in touch with his heart.

So much energy had been pumped into the room that the three of us were feeling much better than we had at the beginning of the session. Carl's body, on the other hand, had begun tightening up. "I'm just feeling that shivering feeling again—very much like fear." He told us that from time to time his body suddenly tensed up this way with fear. When that happened, he didn't feel strong enough to push the fear away. And it had been happening more and more frequently.

Carl had been dealing with the all of these physical issues—the tightening and misery and inflammation—for many years. But it was his fear, rather than his physical symptoms, that alarmed him the most. "Having to try to calm down is pretty difficult."

Robert led us through a healing that did help Carl relax and feel calmer. He was still "a little bit tight," but considerably less tense and afraid.

He told us his right brain just didn't want to open up. Yet he made a connection between starting to get sick many years ago and his first experiences of trying to open up and let the light in. "Right after I had my first (Reiki) attunement, I had a severe crisis with my skin for about a week and a half. Things just kept getting worse after that."

But he told us he'd felt a lot of energy movement today. In fact, he was surprised at how much he'd been able to feel compared to past healings.

Lisa said his auric field was much stronger now, and he would be leaving here in much better shape. Throughout the course of our work with Carl, she had been sending love and light to him at random times, showering him with light whenever she thought of him. She promised to continue doing that. I asked him to let us know how he was doing over the course of the next two weeks, because if we knew what to focus on we could direct healing energy to wherever he needed it at that time. He asked us to "send the calm."

Robert wanted Carl to rest for a few days and allow himself to build up his energy and rejuvenate himself. He had just gone through a major purification and detoxification, so resting was absolutely the best thing he could do. Carl planned to continue working with Margaret after a short hiatus.

A Service for Humanity

We believed our group healings had accomplished what we had been brought together to do. All the entities had been removed from Carl, we had been introduced to the Reptilians, and we had developed a connection with the Arcturians—which was a great blessing. But none of us felt that the work with Carl was finished, and we were open to meeting with him again. Perhaps, however, Carl was now ready to work on issues from this lifetime, and Margaret might be better suited to assist him with that.

There are so many questions about Carl that we'll never get clear and definite answers to. Had his soul made the decision that he would give up his power in this lifetime? Is the point or goal of this life the atonement for his past abuses of power—the crimes he committed and the suffering he caused so many other people? I can't, and don't want to, predict the future, but if that's the case, maybe it isn't in the cards for him to get significantly better. Even if he doesn't experience a radical change in this lifetime, however, all the karma he has healed and is healing will give him a better, fresher start the next time around.

In the meantime, Carl has done a fantastic service for humanity, which may be part of his atonement. He has been a catalyst in my journey, and I personally have a great deal of love and appreciation for him for being willing to show up over and over again and for allowing the rest of us to learn from his extremely difficult and painful situation.

At the very beginning, the message we heard was that Carl was supposed to write a book. Carl was no writer, but even more to the point, his body was so ravaged and he was in so much pain no one could imagine him undertaking a project like writing a book.

Yet two years later, here is this book. This book would not exist were it not for Carl. So what exactly was the message we were hearing? Communications occasionally get garbled in the course of being sent and received—even between humans, but especially between humans and multidimensional beings—and sometimes we translate them incorrectly as they pass through our personal filters. But Carl doesn't have to write a book because the information is right here; it's getting out to the people who need to read it and who can under-stand it and benefit from it.

Carl has done his part in bringing the book to fruition; that task, for him, has been completed.

Chapter 10
Have A Life! Live A Life!

Stories of Positive Outcomes

"Have a life! Live a life!" Alice, whose story is related at the end of this chapter, laughed when she spoke those words. Archangel Michael had just finished removing all the cords that had been wrapped around her, confining her like a straightjacket. Now she was free to start doing just that: living her life.

All the work the healing team had done with Carl has paved the way for some tremendous healings to take place, and I am continually grateful to him for allowing us to work with him and learn from our experiences with him.

These are the stories of four of the many people, who—along with their friends and family members, both living and dead—have benefitted significantly from that work.

Julia: *Make an Investment in Your Spiritual Health*

This is awesome work. I wish everybody would do it—basically clear your own energy and clear other people's stuff, and then

*meet your guides, understand who they are, and then just live it.
It's hard work, but it's an investment. You invest in your physical
health. Why wouldn't you invest in your spiritual health?*

Julia contacted me because she was, in her own words, desperate to
get some relief from the extreme pain she'd been having in her right
hip for several months. She had recently started running again, and
at first she'd thought some strain or injury was causing the pain. By
the time we spoke, however, the pain had spread to the other hip,
and it was so bad she wasn't able to sleep or even lie down. She had
been treated by a chiropractor, had gotten massages, been X-rayed,
tried acupuncture, and attempted to medicate the pain. Nothing had
worked. Supposedly nothing was wrong physically, but the pain
continued to get worse.

She had also been feeling a lot of energy around her that she didn't
think was hers.

*The only way I can describe it is like two magnets when you put
them together. I feel like either something's in my space or I'm
just really out of sorts, which is unusual for me. This last time, I
started hearing voices. I hear things anyway, but these are just
strange—voices that aren't familiar to me. I've been hearing my
name a lot. And I've been having nightmares like you wouldn't
believe.*

When we started working together, she discovered that everything
she'd been experiencing was related. The pain she was feeling
physically was the result of people in her life who were hanging on to
her energetically. Julia also had Reptilians in her, but they had gotten
in fairly recently, and she was in tune with herself and aware enough
to have noticed something had happened.

*When I have them around me, I end up in my house pacing. It's
amazing what it does to me. It's the worst feeling ever.*

We needed to remove the Reptilians before we could do anything else. After they were gone, Julia set a goal for herself of clearing her own space and then learning how to disconnect from the people whose energy she felt had been draining her own. She made a list of those people, starting with family and going on to friends and then even a few people she didn't know personally, but who were friends of friends.

We began with Julia's husband's family, including her mother-in-law, sister-in-law, stepson, and her own children. Her mother-in-law, who was in her 80s, had demons as well as the Reptilian bloodline in her. Julia thought her mother-in-law was afraid to die, but once we removed the bloodline from her, I knew she wouldn't have to fear dying any longer.

Julia had learned a little about the Reptilians from her husband Paul, who had died two years before. She thought he had the bloodline, too, although he fought against its effects. While we were talking about him, I felt his presence. He actually seemed to be leading our healing session; he told me three times that he had guided Julia to me. My guides confirmed Paul did indeed have the Reptilian bloodline. We were able to remove it from him—at the soul level—even though he was deceased. We severed it so that when he reincarnates the next time he will not bring it back with him.

I'd never worked on a deceased spirit before. That was the first time the Arcturians ever did that with me, but they've done it in other cases since then. (You can read more about healing the dead in Chapter 15.) It's actually easier to remove the bloodline imprint from a deceased person than it is from someone still living. Julia thinks the deceased have greater knowledge about these things than we do, and as a result they are probably far more willing to engage in this work. They know that if they get the bloodline removed, it won't come back with them in another incarnation.

After we finished the work on Paul, he wanted us to work on his brother, who was very ill at the time. He then brought in more and more people, and one by one, we removed whatever we could from each of them and cut any negative energetic cords connecting them with Julia. Altogether there were around 20 individuals involved whose energies were, as Julia put it, all twisted up together. She herself did a lot of work on a quite a few people. I was amazed. But she said:

My work was totally selfish. I was just desperate. And I was determined. I was in a lot of pain, and I think that's what happens. You get to a point where you're in physical pain and it's interfering with your life. You're very motivated to do something about it.

One of the people contributing energetically to her hip pain was a very good friend, an "old-soul connection," someone she considers a twin flame.[12] He also had the Reptilian bloodline, and she felt he was connecting to her heart chakra in a negative way. Now she's learned how to open that door to him energetically when she wants to open it—but even more importantly, she knows how to close it.

I actually visualize a door with bolts on it. And I say to myself, "OK, this is closed. It's not appropriate for you to take from me that way." I'm getting better and better at subconsciously opening and closing it when it's appropriate so it's not something I have to be consciously aware of anymore. I'm learning to close off all those unhealthy connections so he can move forward on his path. Because when someone's taking your energy, they're not going anywhere. They're just spinning.

Protecting yourself from someone else's unhealthy energy is obviously good for you, but it can have a positive effect on those around you, as well. If you let someone use your energy or affect it negatively

---

[12] A twin flame or twin soul is the other half of your soul—the yin to your yang, or vice versa—that was separated at the time of physical incarnation. Each flame or soul gains its own experience through multiple physical incarnations. But the deep desire to reunite with your twin is encoded in your DNA.

or siphon it off, you're not doing him or her any favors. We each need to learn how to deal with our own issues.

When Julia started doing this work, it was very intense for her, and the entities harassed her quite a bit.

> *As I was clearing myself and other people, it seemed like a lot of it was coming at me real hard. But once I got through every-thing, it got easier. They leave me alone more.*

Julia recently told me she rarely experiences that pain in her hip now, and when she does have a twinge once in a while early in the morn-ing, she's able to figure out what's causing it. Before, she had been in constant pain; now the pain doesn't last long.

She's still learning to understand and sort out what's hers energeti-cally and what's not hers. When she's uncertain, she intentionally seeks an answer by using a process such as doing a muscle test[13] or having a dialogue with herself.

> *Sometimes it is mine, and that's cool. But just understanding what is and what isn't mine is a big deal. Because that deter-mines how you manage it.*

She's also noticed that when other people's energy occasionally comes in, it goes out very quickly. She doesn't allow it to stick around. It's not a good vibrational match with her anymore.

> *I've cleared those spaces, and I've healed those parts of me that used to allow it. When I feel someone else now, it's like "sorry, off limits." They don't stay.*

---

[13] Muscle testing is a diagnostic aid used by chiropractors, osteopaths, medical doctors, dentists, and other practitioners trained in Applied Kinesiology. You can also learn or be trained to test yourself.

Her husband's brother recently died, and Julia was concerned about being around his family again, especially the people she felt had been siphoning off her energy. But when she went to the funeral, she found that everyone she'd worked with and had cleared felt different to her.

> The interactions felt different. There was no pulling on me. There was no tugging of energy. I felt really well protected. And I felt good about it.

Julia doesn't feel her husband's presence as much as she used to, and when she does feel him, he, too feels different to her. She thinks that since being cleared and then helping us clear his family, he has moved on to doing other things.

She continues to call on the Arcturians for protection, and she has accepted their download. She considers them "the big guns" and regularly asks them to protect her property. Her house is on a lake on Native American land, and she describes the area as having "just tons of energy on a good day." There had been a Reptilian portal in her attic that we were able to remove and which a psychic has confirmed is still gone. So Julia's now doing an extremely good job of protecting her space, internally and externally.

> I'm not getting the energy attacks from other people. Before, they would find their way in through the dream state, or if I was having a vulnerable moment, they'd be right there. But that isn't happening anymore. I think everybody's tired of me. They're tired of that door I've shut. So it's like, "You know what? Move on."

Darlene: *Third-Dimensional Technologies Can't Resolve Multidimensional Issues*

> *I knew that going to a psychiatrist or a psychologist wasn't going to help me in the long run. They would probably medicate me and use third-dimensional technologies, but honestly they really don't have a clue that what's causing these problems in most people are multidimensional issues.*

Darlene was one of the handful of people I worked on who didn't immediately have the kind of results both of us were hoping to see. She came to me because she had been experiencing severe anxiety, something that was relatively new to her. She had seen a psychiatrist and was taking antidepressant medication, but since she believed her problems came from the spiritual realm, she didn't have a great deal of confidence in traditional medicine.

> *When I first came to see you I was really sick. I was very jumpy, very anxious, very upset, and I was really desperate to find a cure. I knew that the mental problems I was having were spiritually based. I didn't understand what I had, but I knew I wasn't going to find peace or solace or a cure from a physician. And I didn't, either. I feel lucky that at least I had this path to try or this hunch to go on. Most people have no knowledge of it, and so they suffer and don't get better until they have a spiritual cure.*

As it turned out, her intuition was very good. She's right; many people, maybe the majority, don't realize they have entities inside them, whether it's demons or discarnates or Reptilians. But some people like Darlene are more intuitive or aware, and they sense there's something there. They know something's wrong, although they may have no idea what it is.

My first two sessions with Darlene, which were close together, occurred before I knew anything about the Reptilians or about my connection with the Arcturians. We did remove some entities, and in each of those two sessions, she felt there had been a healing and a release. One was quite powerful.

> *The release was really strong. It felt like a gust of wind had left my body. It was like opening a soft drink bottle and releasing the air from the vacuum.*

In spite of the healing that had taken place, Darlene continued to suffer from debilitating anxiety and bouts of depression for the next year.

> *I was struggling at work, and I kept my job somehow, but then I ended up in the hospital for five days. I had a nervous break-down.*

In cases when people don't show improvement, it may be due to a multiplicity of complex issues or because they aren't willing to do the work they need to do. Darlene, however, was doing her best to try to remove the blocks through any means available. She had been meditating for years as best she could. Yet even though we had removed those entities and she was making a considerable effort on her own behalf, she still wasn't getting well. Darlene was really a classic case in this regard. If you are trying to remove entities from someone but you don't know about Reptilians, you won't know to look for them. You may think you've finished clearing that person, but you haven't.

Although she felt marginally better than she had before she came to see me the first two times, Darlene was obviously still quite misera-ble. By the third time we met, I had become familiar with the Reptili-ans, and I knew how to call in the Arcturians. Right away, I saw that

Darlene had Reptilians in her. They were the source of her anxiety. Interestingly, Darlene had learned of the Reptilians on her own.

I knew about the Reptilians before I came to see you. I knew that they existed, but I never thought they were inside of me because I'd been meditating for the past 15 years.

She had been maintaining her spiritual practices for a long time and thought she was being purified and protected by them. So she was shocked to find out she had entities attached to her and in her.

Her sickness got a little worse before it got better. Like many others, she felt the most discomfort during her initial struggle, when the Reptilians were trying to keep their hooks in her and she was fighting to get rid of them. Her healing was a process, as is everyone's. It took time for her to release all the negative energy she had been carrying around with her. But after we removed the Reptilians, her anxiety completely disappeared, and she remains free of it today. Now she's able to make the positive changes she was struggling to make when she was still trying to function with Reptilians in her.

Since the anxiety has left me, I have a job that I really enjoy and am doing very well at. Before it was always difficult for me to work because I was anxious, and I was sick a lot. I moved out into my own apartment, too. I'm much more stable, not going from place to place. I've been in the same place for a year. Everything has settled down. Everything is going well. Everything's a hundred percent better. I'm a lot lighter.

It's easy to see the difference in Darlene now. She's obviously much more at peace. But she's taking an active role in doing her own work; she isn't being passive. She's doing what she needs to do in order to keep things in her life settled and "going well."

I'm clearing up all my old business, all the loose ends in my life. I'm sorting them out and clearing them up. I used to channel and I enjoyed it, but I haven't been doing it for the past few months because I've had a full-time job and a part-time job. I'm going to start getting back into it now. I'm going to do it much more personally, like a research project, to get information and deal with my higher self mainly, just for my own growth.

I was curious about how Darlene had been able to meditate before she had the entities removed since they tend to block people from connecting with Source and with the higher self. Many people I work worth tell me they can't really meditate until after the entities are gone. Darlene said meditation has never been easy for her, partly because it requires discipline.

It's like exercise. I like the results of meditation, so I stick with it. But I am able to meditate more easily now. I don't have as many thoughts jumping around in my head.

More than a year after the work we did, Darlene is doing better on all levels: physical, mental, emotional, and spiritual.

I'm really grateful for your help and that I got rid of these entities. I don't think they're coming back. I'm just happy to be moving forward. I appreciate the help of the Arcturians and all the beings who are helping us. It's been really positive for me.

Veronica: *Please Help Me Find a Way to Help My Sister*

My sister was in the worst state imaginable for so very long. She went from being absolutely tortured, where every minute felt like days and every day felt like years, to being happy, to having her life back. What you've done for me and my family is just so amazing. And I'm so thankful.

Veronica contacted me on behalf of her younger sister, Amy, who had spent a night in a haunted hotel room where, unbeknownst to her, someone had been murdered. The hotel staff knew about the murder, but no one told her. Amy discovered the information on her own after the fact. But even though she didn't know about the murder at the time, she knew something really bad had happened to her while she had stayed in that room.

She came back saying that she was possessed. It was terrible. She seemed to get better, but that was very short-lived. Soon she started avoiding the whole family, staying away from everybody. And she would make comments to me that something was going on, but she couldn't tell me what it was. It was too dangerous. She said she didn't want anything bad to happen to me. When she broke down and told me we had to call the FBI and the CIA, I knew things had gotten much worse than I'd imagined.

Amy hadn't had any of these issues prior to staying in that hotel room. Her boyfriend used marijuana, and he persuaded her to use it that night. She was also taking Adderall, which is used to treat ADHD, and she smoked cigarettes. Veronica thinks the drugs weakened Amy's auric shield and allowed those entities to get into her, which is something I've seen happen over and over again. Using just one drug, whether it's prescription or illegal, can lower your vibrational frequency, but when you start piling them up like that, it can quickly take your vibration all the way down to the bottom.

Amy gradually stopped smiling or laughing altogether, and her life became more and more constricted. It got to the point where she wasn't able to be alone, wouldn't drive or use the computer or watch TV. She wouldn't even talk on her cell phone. She started sleeping with her mother every night.

Because she was hearing voices, her family took her to see a psychiatrist, and he diagnosed her with psychosis, a severe mental disorder, and prescribed medication for her. But Veronica was never convinced that was the whole story—or that she and her family were helpless to find some other type of relief for Amy.

She wanted help. I could see it in her eyes. She couldn't do it on her own, but I always knew there was something we could do. It was like a gut instinct. But I didn't know how or what. So I just kept asking and praying, "Please lead me to the right people, places, and things that will help me help my sister."

Although Veronica was referred to a number of different healers and practitioners, none of them felt right to her, and she didn't follow up with any of them.

Then I found out about you, Wayne, and it took everything I had to call you, but I knew I had to. And almost immediately after I talked to you, I knew you could help her. I was scared, and I didn't know everything that was going on, but there was something about you. I knew you were trustworthy and that you could help her. That's really all it was.

As soon as we started working together, Veronica realized Amy wasn't just hearing voices. There were actual entities inside her sister, tormenting her and threatening to hurt or kill everyone around her. Veronica told me the various entities in Amy seemed to harass her in unique ways. One of them told her she wasn't allowed to sit on a particular red couch. Once that entity was removed, Amy was able to sit on the couch again.

Amy had a lot of entities in her—demons, discarnates, Reptilians, and attachments. So just as with Carl, there were many layers that had to be peeled away. Amy wasn't even aware we were doing this work to remove these entities from her. But her soul gave permission for us to do it. I've never yet had a soul deny permission for one of these healings. And even though Amy wasn't present and knew nothing about our work, the results were clearly visible to Veronica.

Amy showed signs of improvement after just one session. It's been a gradual process, a slow process, because she doesn't know what's been going on. She doesn't realize it, but I've seen so many signs of improvement since these things were removed. I would be sitting next to her, and when I looked into her eyes, it was like she wasn't there. And then all of a sudden I could see her again. I could see it in her eyes. She went from being tortured one minute, to the next minute being peaceful again.

Since the Reptilians and all the other entities have been removed, Amy has quit smoking, and she's now driving again and doing all those things she was afraid to do before. She has an opportunity to reclaim her life, and she's taking advantage of it.

Veronica herself has never had Reptilians in her. She has a very bright light and she works to keep herself clean and well-protected. Her connections with her guides and angels have grown much stronger, and her vibration is higher. She's connected with the Arcturians now, too, and has accepted their download.

I ask for protection many times a day, and ask for my family and myself to be surrounded by the Arcturians' protective light and by Archangel Michael's protective warrior angels. And they do. They protect us all the time.

As soon as she senses something coming at her, trying to get in, she calls in her team and has it removed. When she doesn't think she can remove it herself, she gets in touch with me, because she knows these entities and attachments won't go away by themselves. They have to be taken to the Light.

You and your team saved my life on multiple occasions. I felt the Reptilians surrounding me, literally trying to choke me. I felt like I was suffocating. I got in touch with you, and I could tell the instant they were removed because in a matter of seconds I went from feeling surrounded by these terrible things to feeling surrounded by love.

All that peace and love is the Arcturians coming through, along with Jesus, Archangel Michael, Archangel Raphael, and the angels. When I call in that team and we release something negative from someone's energy field, they fill that space with love and peace. They just pour it in.

Veronica called me late one evening when she was being attacked. As soon as she described what was happening, I called in my guides, and I saw a huge python wrapping itself around her. That meant Reptilians at the very highest level, the Draconian level, were attacking her. It was an indication they were pretty serious about her. We removed it immediately, but I'll never forget it.

Veronica is actually grateful for these experiences that most of us would consider negative. She says they have allowed her to relate to someone who has been possessed. That's remarkable to me. She is truly an empathetic soul. Maybe the Arcturians did want her to have those experiences. Sometimes they'll let something slip through to me so I can understand what it feels like. I don't like it. Not at all. But Veronica knows now that whatever is bothering her will be taken to the Light. She will be OK.

You literally have given my sister her life back. And you have given me this sense of absolute peace and freedom that's almost indescribable. You can't put a price on it. It's so amazing, and it means the world to me. I'm so thankful for that.

Alice: *Have a Life! Live a Life!*

I can see it's been in our family. I just feel it. And for me, the theme of my whole life has been feeling disconnected. I know I'm a spiritual person, so it's been just horrible because I've felt held down. It's hard to get to that other vibration because it's like having chains on you all the time.

I had my first session with Alice a few days after she had seen David Icke[14] in person, in Australia, where she lives. She told me he had put into words a lot of what she had already been feeling. She was glad she saw him before our session because it clarified several things for her.

I removed some demons from her almost immediately, and then I felt some neck pain which indicated Reptilians. Sure enough, she had them, although they were not in her bloodline. I asked the Arcturians to remove them and everything associated with them.

It was interesting Alice had used the word "chains," because I sensed a lot of cords wrapped around her. She had so many cords, in fact, that Archangel Michael used his sword to cut them, wielding it like a surgical knife, taking it straight up through all of them. When he cut those cords, it was as if he were cutting open a straightjacket. All of those cords were taken to the Light. Afterward, Alice actually said she felt like she'd been released from a straightjacket and now she wanted to take off in life and fly.

She had been incredibly bound up, and while living her life had always been a challenge, it had been especially hard for her over the past five years.

I got really sick. I think it's an infection in my gums, but nothing shows up. Every test comes back normal. It's really affected my brain and my emotions. I get so anxious. I've always been sort of anxious and afraid, but I got really worse and could no longer control it. I had to give up my job. I couldn't focus or concentrate or remember. I haven't worked for about four years. I'm at a

---

14 David Icke is a British writer and speaker who has written and lectured extensively on the Reptilians and the ways in which they have infiltrated all major power structures and are currently controlling humanity.

point where I need to do something, but I don't know what to do. There's that disconnection all the time, like a boat without a rudder.

Now that the Reptilians had been removed, I was sure Alice would find she did have a rudder. She was opened up in a way she hadn't been her whole life. I recommended some meditation tools for her to use so she could make that connection with Source she'd been trying to make for such a long time.

Alice was living temporarily with one of her sisters and wanted me to check her sister's house. I didn't find any portals or any Reptilians inside the house, but there was a discarnate—a ghost—that my guides removed and took to the Light. Alice was amazed. She told me there had been two children in the house that morning, one of whom was very sensitive, and the two were playing ghosts. Was that a coincidence?

When I checked Alice's sister, she turned out to have the Reptilian bloodline, which the Arcturians removed. She did not seem to have any demons, however, which was unusual. Alice said her sister was psychic, so maybe she had had some sort of healing to remove them. Alice had always been frightened of both her sisters, and she didn't think she'd be able to talk to them about the Reptilians. But she was wrong. The sister whose house Alice was staying in had actually seen the ghost we removed sitting and reading the newspaper. That was enough verification for her, and it made her more receptive.

Later on, Alice found out her sister knew about the Reptilians and had felt their energy in herself. She told Alice she'd always hated her skin because she felt it was like the skin of a lizard. Quite a few other people who have had Reptilians in them have also had skin issues, including Carl, who had severe eczema.

Being able to talk about their experiences with the Reptilians brought Alice and her sister closer together.

One of Alice's greatest concerns was her relationship with her son. Alice and her ex-husband had not been married long when their son was born, and they separated when he was three or four years old. Alice moved out of the area with her son to keep him away from what she perceived as the dark influence of his father. Now, however, her son, who was in his 20s, seemed to be falling under that influence.

One of his stepsisters died just over a year ago. As a result, he sort of turned against me. I feel as though he's been taken in by what I feel is darkness.

Her son had the Reptilian bloodline, which he hadn't gotten from Alice, so we thought it may have come from his father. The Arcturians removed it, along with one or two attachments, sending all of them to the Light. In addition to the entities, he had a lot of negative thought forms, which I sensed as being black and dark, like gunk. Negative thought forms can become entity-like over time. When we remove them, the angels turn them into what looks like a dark rope, and they pull it out through the crown chakra and take it to the Light. If those negative thought forms aren't removed, they become hard and calcified, like bricks. At that stage, they're not impossible to break up—my guides have done it a number of times—but it's more difficult to do.

Clearly, the Reptilians did not want Alice and her son to connect. That was the biggest barrier between them, but now that it was being removed, they would finally have a chance to do that. Although her son had had the Reptilian bloodline, he was young. He hadn't had as many years of being bombarded by them as Alice's sister had. Yes, he'd been brainwashed by all the negative influences surrounding him, but I felt more confident he would rebound.

When I talked with Alice a month later, her infection was healing, she hadn't picked up any more entities, and she was working! Her son had reached out to her, too, shortly after our session. Alice still had issues to deal with, which was to be expected, but the difference was that she *was* dealing with them.

> *My head is becoming clearer. I'm still really anxious sometimes, particularly in regard to my teaching, because I've never seen myself as a great teacher. But I think I'm better now than I have been. I just want to relax and be who I am. That's what I still struggle with. My experience has been that I've often been attacked when I put out who I really am. So I'm always a bit hesitant to share what I really think.*

Since she was teaching in a different geographical location, she was no longer living with her sister, but she reported that her sister was doing much better, too.

> *Her life had been going from one disaster to the next. Now she has been able to do things—getting papers in order, particularly around her husband's investments—that she hasn't been able to do for five years. Life has started moving, instead of being this hard grind it has always been.*

Because she didn't think her ex-husband's energy was very good, Alice wanted me to check him. Although she felt a karmic connection with him and thought the two of them had had previous lifetimes together, they were incompatible in this lifetime. She really loved him, however, and hadn't had another partner since separating from him.

> *I was devastated we didn't stay together, but I've had a lot of growing up to do in life. I've always felt the connection between us, and I was heartbroken that this lifetime we haven't managed to be together. He's been very dark, but underneath all that there is that good energy. So who knows what will happen.*

The Arcturians confirmed he did have Reptilians in him, but he did not have the bloodline. Since Alice's son had the bloodline, but neither of his parents had it, it may have skipped a generation. Or he may have had the bloodline in a past life and died with it still imprinted on his soul. That's why it's so extremely important to remove it no matter how old the person is and even if he or she is no longer alive, as was the case with Julia's husband. If the bloodline isn't removed, the person's soul will keep bringing it back into each incarnation. In this situation, since Alice's son was born with the bloodline, he may have affected one or both of his parents. So this can go in either direction. Yes, the bloodline follows the maternal or paternal line—or in some cases both—but once you have it, it stays with you forever. It doesn't end when this lifetime ends. It endures. It has to be removed in order for it to go away.

Alice's ex-husband also had a couple of demons. All of those entities—demons and Reptilians and everything else—like to destroy families and family relationships. So it's no surprise this family was fragmented.

Her ex-husband had remarried shortly after Alice separated from him, so I also checked his wife. She did not have Reptilians in her, but she did have some around her that were harassing her, and we got rid of them.

Alice felt that her ex-husband and his wife and their children were not very awake or aware. It was possible the healings she'd just facilitated would help them awaken. It certainly couldn't hurt them. Now it was up to them to walk their own paths, deal with their own karmic issues, and learn on their own.

When entities are removed from people, the healing not only removes whatever blocks are there, it also raises their vibrational frequency. That affects the people around them, too, especially the family members they live with. All of this helps raise the vibration of this planet, as well. So it isn't just the one person who's being cleared that's affected. Every time we can get rid of an entity—whether it's a demon, a discarnate, or a Reptilian—the vibration of this planet gets just a little bit higher.

Alice's son had a long-time girlfriend with whom Alice had a good relationship. She wasn't expecting me to find anything in her, but it was good we checked because she had bloodline Reptilians, too. I told Alice to give herself a pat on the back for thinking of checking her son's girlfriend, since her son would probably have been influenced by the Reptilians in her.

Alice's journey is not over, of course, but she is well on her way to having her life back, and living it well.

> I am reflecting on things and using them as an opportunity to learn by seeing aspects of myself in the behavior of others. I feel so different than I did before our first session. It is so good to be free of that energy. And I continue to focus on building my connection with the divine part of myself.

Long-Distance Healing

Of the four people profiled in this chapter, I only worked with one face-to-face. I've had many people tell me they don't believe in long-distance, remote healing. They insist on seeing me in person. A few people who live in other countries have wanted to make expensive and complicated travel arrangements to come to Albuquerque to see me. But if you know you have entities inside you, why would you want to keep them in there any longer than you have to? It's not necessary to wait. It's not necessary to do this in person. There was no difference in the quality or the effectiveness of the healings in these four people. Whether remotely, or in person, all were helped. All had positive results.

And the positive results weren't just for themselves, but also for their families and friends. At least 90% of the people I work on are like

Veronica's sister, Amy, or Julia's in-laws, or Alice's ex-husband—people who don't necessarily know they're getting a healing.

The vast majority of people who contact me directly, and who follow up by doing their own work, have very good outcomes. Although there are similarities, each person is unique; each situation is a little different. But when it comes to removing Reptilians, there's only one answer, and it's the same in every single case: the Arcturians.

PART THREE

Chapter 11
Arcturians, Reptilians, and You

Who Has Reptilians?

Not everyone has Reptilians, and many people who do are either in denial or are reluctant to acknowledge it or talk about it. If you suspect you are one of the people who have them, I can't emphasize enough that the most powerful force available to help you with them—really the *only* force—is the Arcturians. They have dominion over the Reptilians. I'm not aware of anyone other than the Arcturians who can remove Reptilians and keep you protected from them afterward.

Only about half of the people I've worked with who have demons or discarnates also have Reptilians, but nearly everyone who has Reptilians also has demons and/or discarnates. The signs and symptoms for possession by any of these entities are very similar and were outlined in Chapter 2. The Reptilians are so subtle—or maybe devious is a better way to describe them—they are not easy to single out and detect. Having a lot of nightmares or dreams that include snakes, particularly if they're large snakes, is one possible indicator they're there. And if you're experiencing recurring headaches, such as migraines, or chronic neck or shoulder problems or skin issues, that's another sign you may have Reptilians.

Of course, demons can also cause all kinds of physical problems including headaches and neck and shoulder pain, so you really won't know whether it's Reptilians until a healer goes in to remove something and finds them. That can be difficult, too, because the Reptilians are able to put a veil or a force field around themselves, a shield they hide behind. If the psychic or intuitive healer or anyone else who is trying to remove the entities doesn't call in the Arcturians, they can very easily miss the Reptilians. Time and time again, healers have told me, "OK, we've cleared that person; we're done." They think they're finished, but they're not because the Reptilians are still there, probably along with a few more demons and discarnates, too. But they weren't even aware of the Reptilians.

Reptilians are able to control demons, and they can shield them from view when we're trying to remove them. In my experience, the demons usually go first during removal. But sometimes as soon as I start to remove them, all of a sudden I can't sense them anymore. The Reptilians will sacrifice some demons and try to lull me into believing the job is done, which is exactly what they did when I started working with Carl. They blocked me from sensing them and kept me from being able to tell exactly what was in him. Now I call on the Arcturians immediately to come in and neutralize the Reptilians so they'll stop shielding the demons and we can get on with our work. Once the Reptilians are exposed and removed, other demons and the discarnates are able to go.

How Do They Get In?

Reptilians can get into you the same way demons or discarnates do. When a single Reptilian (or demon or discarnate) gets into you, the effects may be subtle enough that you don't pick up on it right away.

Often the situation gets progressively worse before you realize *something* keeps getting in your way. But some discarnates also have demons and Reptilians in them, and they bring those other entities with them when they get into you. All of a sudden, you have a whole passel of entities to deal with. When you take on a lot of different entities at the same time, it usually hits you hard. You're likely to notice something's amiss. Your family and friends and coworkers may notice changes in you, too. Because the effects are so dramatic, you're more likely to seek help sooner, and your chances of having a positive outcome once everything has been removed are usually good.

Unlike demons and discarnates, Reptilians have another way to get into you besides coming in directly or piggybacking on discarnates, and that is through your bloodline. If they're in your bloodline, they are present in your DNA from the time you are born and their genetic code is already activated. Bloodline Reptilians are more difficult to deal with. Yes, they're a little bit harder to remove, but the bigger issue is that if you have the bloodline, you don't know what it's like not to have this gang of entities inside you carrying on a 24/7 block party. You never noticed a difference when they entered you, because they were always in you. You have no idea what life is like without them, what it's like to just be *you*. Sure, you have your own mind, your own self or psyche, but it's competing with maybe two or three demons, three Reptilians, and a discarnate or two. That's why Carl had such a difficult time even after the Reptilians and all the other entities and attachments were removed. Some of them had always been in him. That was his status quo. Although he certainly wasn't happy about the situation, having them was a part of his identity. How could it have been any other way?

The Reptilians can follow either the maternal bloodline or the paternal bloodline or even both. I'm not 100% certain how they get into the bloodline, but I do know that when people have the bloodline, their lives are much more challenging—both before and after the Reptilians are removed.

I believe that nearly everyone on this planet actually has some Reptilian genetic material as part of their DNA, but unless you have the bloodline, that genetic material, or genetic code, remains dormant until it's activated. If you have Reptilians in you, the Reptilian genetic code *has* been activated. I don't know whether they activate the genetic code first and then go in, or go in and then activate it. The genetic code can also get activated under conditions of extreme stress and trauma, such as physical or sexual abuse.

While all these different entities are destructive by nature, not all of them are messing around with you at the chromosome level, and not all of them have an organized agenda like the Reptilians have. The Reptilians are not only organized and controlled, they're intent on taking you over and using you as they see fit in order to fulfill their agenda. The Reptilians don't care about *you*, personally, or what *you* want or care about or aspire to. You're nothing but a tool or slave to them. If you listen to them long enough, you may start buying into what they're trying to get you to do and to believe. You may forget who you really are and everything that's important and meaningful to you.

Turning to the Arcturians

It may get to the point where it seems easier to stop trying to fight them and to simply give in. But that's the worst thing you can possibly do. You don't want to give in to them. Once you've made that decision, once you've consciously accepted them, it's much, much harder to remove them. You won't need just one session; you'll need a lot of sessions, because as soon as we try to remove them, they will start pulling out all the stops. So whatever you do, don't give up or give in in to the Reptilians. You have an alternative. The Arcturians *will* help you.

I can't say this too many times: if you want to be free of Reptilians, it's absolutely essential that you develop and maintain a personal connection with the Arcturians. Jesus isn't going to remove the

Reptilians; Archangel Michael isn't going to do it; the rest of the archangels and the Ascended Masters aren't going to do it. The Pleiadians and others will assist and help provide protection, but it's the Arcturians who remove and keep the Reptilians at bay. And as I've also said many times, they work through me and through other people who have been trained, but they're the ones actually doing the work.

When the Arcturians remove the Reptilians, those individual Reptilians are gone for good. They go to the Light, and they don't come back. The Arcturians take them up and out right through the crown chakra, one after another. As it's happening, the Reptilians don't seem to understand they're goners because nothing has bothered them for millions of years.

I've never seen anyone pick up Reptilians again after they've been removed. It just doesn't happen. But that doesn't mean Reptilians can't still get to you and cause you all kinds of trouble from the periphery. I assure you they do not give up easily. They've enlisted many demons to carry out their orders, so even though they may not be able to get back into you after they've been removed, they can send in demons to do their dirty work. First they fight to hang on, and then they fight to try to regain whatever they've lost.

Eggs, Not Seeds

One of their last-ditch efforts to keep their tentacles or hooks in you is to leave eggs behind as the Arcturians are whisking them away. When we first saw this happening with Carl and several other people, we weren't exactly sure what it was we were seeing. Were they seeds? Finally, one of the psychics got it. They're not seeds; they're eggs! The Reptilians leave eggs behind, which makes sense. Clearing out all those eggs is a crucial part of the clean-up process. They all have to go. Any that are left behind will allow the Reptilians to be reborn inside you. As long as we ask the Arcturians to remove them, the eggs are easy to clean up. The Arcturians can suck them right up as if they were wielding some kind of cosmic vacuum cleaner.

If the Reptilians are in you, you will have an etheric homing device or chip in your DNA that needs to be disabled. If the homing device is present, it's already been activated, and even after the Reptilians have been removed, it acts like an energetic or etheric cord connecting you to I-don't-know-where. Reptilian headquarters? Once they begin the process, it takes the Arcturians three weeks to disable the homing device and reconfigure your genetic code and your DNA. Removing the Reptilians does not immediately remove that energetic cord connecting you to Reptilian headquarters, so you will still be under their control to some extent. The Reptilians will continue to harass and interfere with you as much as they can during that three-week period.

By reconfiguring your DNA, the Arcturians very lovingly create the opportunity for you to reprogram yourself. They remove the negative influence of the Reptilians, and they give you some breathing room. They make it possible for you to do the work you need to do. But unless you do that work and reprogram yourself—develop some positive connections for positive influences—you're likely to stay stuck in the same old negative and self-destructive patterns.

Lifting Yourself Up

Possession affects you on every level: physical, emotional, mental, and spiritual. Reprogramming yourself after you've had Reptilians or other entities affecting your thinking is no different than the reprogramming you would need to do if you had a drug or alcohol addiction. Even if you stop using the drug, the thinking patterns that were a part of your drug use most likely have created a few problems in your life that won't clear up by themselves. You'll need to identify the problem areas in your life and come up with ways to address and solve them. You'll also need to monitor your thinking patterns and learn how to change negative thinking into positive thinking. If you need help, don't be afraid to seek it out and use it.

You may have tried numerous times to do these things before but felt blocked, and that may have left you feeling frustrated and incapable. Now that the Reptilians are no longer blocking you, you have much greater freedom and control. Take advantage of it. It's all too easy to relapse back to drug and alcohol use if you don't change your thinking and deal with your problems. The same is true with possession. If you continue your old thinking patterns and don't do your work, you create a fertile ground for demons, discarnates, and attachments to get back into you and for Reptilians to attack and harass you. If you aren't paying attention, there are all kinds of ways you may unwittingly lay out the welcome mat for these entities and open yourself up to more trouble from them.

Without exception, everyone who has had any of these entities, especially Reptilians, initially has a very low vibrational frequency. When you've had all that mind chatter going on and your vibrational frequency is bottoming out, it's almost impossible to slow down and quiet your mind. People complain about this to me all the time. "I can't meditate. Not even for 30 seconds." They may have taken meditation classes and tried all sorts of techniques, but they simply could not do it. It's hard to gain perspective on your life when you can't even sit still for a few minutes. And it's very difficult to have a connection with Source when you have no connection with yourself. You need to take the time, put in the effort, and make it a priority to do your reprogramming. You can learn how to raise your vibrational frequency in the next chapter, but *you* have to do it. No one else can do it for you.

Remember that none of this is going to happen overnight. Depending on how long you've had Reptilians and whether or not you have the bloodline, it could take a moderate amount of time and effort or it could take a great deal of time and effort to reprogram yourself. Having entities removed is an opportunity, just like winning the lottery is an opportunity. How many people are convinced winning the lottery would solve all their problems? And how many people who do win the lottery end up no better off than they were before because they didn't use the opportunity wisely? It's up to you to make good use of the opportunities you're presented with. Removal alone is not the silver bullet many people are hoping to find.

Closing All Portals

Even after they are no longer in you, and the eggs have been removed and the homing device disabled, the Reptilians can still harangue and annoy you if there are open portals near you. There are portals throughout the entire universe that extraterrestrials use for inter-dimensional travel, but the ones we're concerned with here are the vast network of underground portals and caverns or bases the Reptilians have created on Earth and in which they live. The Reptili-ans travel through these portals, which have points of entry and exit inside buildings. These portal openings allow the Reptilians to come and go freely so they can annoy and harass you and maybe your family, too—even your pets—and create a lot of dark, chaotic energy within your home or workplace. About half the people I've seen who have Reptilians also have one or more portals somewhere nearby. So when we're clearing out the Reptilians, we always try to make certain there are no open portals they can use, especially in living and work spaces.

The Arcturians don't simply close off a portal immediately. If they did that, the Reptilians that are down there would just find another access route. Instead the Arcturians first send a shaft of light, a vortex, into that portal and follow the portal down as far as it goes, which could be a short distance or all the way into the center of the earth.

This is the same shaft of light they use when they're removing the Reptilians from you, but it in that case it's a very gentle and loving shaft of light. When they're creating a vortex and sending the light down into a portal, it's an active, energetic, swirling shaft of light. It's not a little ray or beam of sunshine. Think of the energy a tornado has. It's that kind of energy. It's that powerful. It sucks up whatever is down there and pulls it out. The Arcturians remove every single Reptilian from that portal. They neutralize them. It's as if they're stunned. Depending on how deep the portal is, the Arcturians may keep that vortex going for a few hours or for several days or even weeks. Only after all the Reptilians are gone do they finally close the portal and seal it up.

In some cases, I've found portals inside people. These are extremely tiny portals called "pinprick" portals that are actually openings in the auric shield. But the Reptilians don't need those pinprick portals to get into people. It's usually demons or sometimes attachments that use them. Still, we want to close off the pinprick portals, too, so that nothing has easy access to you.

Once the Arcturians have finished their work, which is really **the first part of the healing process**, you are in a position to continue the healing yourself by developing good habits to protect yourself. The single most important thing you can do in that regard is connect with the Arcturians, not just once, but regularly, consistently. Maintain your connection with them. Keep calling on them. If you don't do it, the Reptilians will still be able to interfere in your life by harassing you from the periphery. They will put up a shield or force field similar to the one they put around themselves and the demons that were inside you. The shield can't be penetrated without the assistance of the Arcturians, so the Reptilians can conceal themselves from anyone who doesn't call on the Arcturians.

Accepting the Arcturian Download

If it feels right to you, call the Arcturians in and ask for and accept their download. It isn't painful; in fact, for most people it's a very calm, loving, and peaceful experience. But you may not feel anything at all. It only takes a few seconds, and it puts you on their radar screen. I don't fully understand how it works, but some kind of an energetic exchange takes place. It helps them protect you, and it helps them communicate with you and you with them. I suggest people contact them and ask for their protection on a daily basis.

I used to find it a bit disconcerting that we had to keep asking them for help and protection. Why can't we ask just once and be done with it? But no form of psychic or spiritual protection works that way. Think of it as developing good psychic habits to take care of your spiritual self the same way you develop good exercise and eating habits to take care of your physical self. The Arcturians are very good, very powerful, extreme protectors. They want to help you, but they can't unless you ask. Reptilians and demons don't care what you want. They'll violate your free will and put thoughts into your head that aren't yours. The Arcturians will never do anything like that. They are karmic beings, as we are, and they honor the universal laws.

The Battle Between the Darkness and the Light

As I said in Chapter 4, I don't believe any more Reptilians are coming here, but they do continue to breed. A few may still be flying around out there trying to get past the starship Athena to get to us here on Earth. The Arcturians have talked about several races of malevolent extraterrestrials that tried to take them on all at the same time since they knew they wouldn't be able to do it individually. They tried to destroy the starship Athena, but that failed so I doubt many of them even attempt it anymore. Right now the Arcturians and other positive, loving extraterrestrials are continuing to block a lot of different dark-force extraterrestrials from coming here.

The Reptilians already here are doing everything they can to destroy us. They want to keep us in this third-dimensional density where we're bombarded with negativity and constantly forced to fight them off and fight off all these other things—demons, discarnates, cords, attachments, and everything else. They want to keep our vibrational frequency as low as possible.

The Arcturians, on the other hand, are doing everything within their power to neutralize the Reptilians and to assist us in raising our vibrational frequency. The Arcturians are able to see so much more than we can see. They don't have the limitations we third-dimensional humans do, and they've been around for so much longer that their perspective is broader than ours could possibly be. If you call on these loving and benevolent, yet extremely intelligent and powerful beings, they can keep the Reptilians away and keep you free from their control. But you have to want their help. You have to ask for it. You have to choose to use it.

Chapter 12
Vibration and Protection

Strengthening Your Auric Shield

Your aura is the luminous electromagnetic energy field that surrounds your physical body like a shield and radiates outward. It arises from the multiple electromagnetic fields of your chakras, and it changes shape and color to reflect your physical, emotional, mental, and spiritual well-being.

Your auric shield also reflects your vibrational frequency. When your vibrational frequency is high, your auric shield is more likely to be strong and intact. When your vibrational frequency is low, your auric shield can more easily become weak and even fractured, making it that much easier for entities such as demons, discarnates, or Reptilians, as well as cords and attachments, to penetrate it and get through to you.

Raising your vibrational frequency strengthens your auric shield. A strong auric shield is absolutely the best protection you can possibly have against entities, attachments, and cords, as well as against other people's negative thoughts and feelings.

In Chapter 1, I related what happened the very first time I was involved in removing an entity from someone. After the demon left Maria, who had been its host—and before I realized I have to send these things to the Light when I remove them and not just set them loose—it tried to get into me by penetrating my auric shield. I actually felt it trying to break through in several different places. Fortunately, my auric shield was strong enough to protect me. I was already aware that having a strong auric shield was important, but in that moment I got a lesson in exactly *how* important it is.

The two crucial things to remember are:

1. *Maintaining a strong auric shield is the best way to protect yourself.*

2. *Raising your vibrational frequency is the best way to strengthen your auric shield.*

Raising Your Vibration

Everything in the universe is in motion, whether solid, liquid, or gas. All things move, vibrate, and travel in circular patterns. Each thing that exists is identified by its own unique vibrational frequency.

Dr. Norma Milanovich and Dr. Shirley McCune
The Light Shall Set You Free

Everything is connected and everything vibrates. Physical matter—what we experience through our five senses—is dense and vibrates at a lower frequency. Color vibrates within the visible spectrum of light from red to violet. Red vibrates at the lowest frequency, and violet vibrates at the highest frequency. Ultraviolet, which we are unable to see with the naked eye, vibrates at an even higher frequency. Our thoughts, feelings, and desires also vibrate at various frequencies, and we send out our vibrations into the universe. Vibrations at the lower level or frequency—such as an angry outburst, for example—don't generally last long, but they have a stronger short-term effect. Higher vibrations, which are subtler than lower vibrations, have the longest-lasting effect. The Arcturians tell us that our own vibrational frequency draws to us whatever lies within that frequency.

Since our planet resides in the third dimension, its vibrational frequency is much lower and denser than the vibrational frequency of the higher dimensions. El Morya says, "The mission is to move from the plane of dense matter and duality up to the plane of Oneness."[15] Our personal vibrations can actually help to either raise or lower the entire planet's vibrations.

On a personal level, our vibrational frequency also affects the people around us just as other people's vibrations affect us. Each thought, word, feeling, and behavior resides on its own frequency. Optimism, for example, resides on a higher frequency; pessimism and cynicism reside on lower frequencies. It is in our best interest to pay attention to what we're putting out and what we're taking in. A vibration of anger or fear in one person may create a similar vibration in someone else. The same is true of higher vibrations. If we are vibrating at a high frequency, we are sending love out into the universe—and love is the highest vibration of all.

We can choose positive thoughts, feelings, and behaviors that raise our vibration and help us advance along the spiritual path. Or we can choose negative thoughts, feelings, and behaviors that lower our vibrations. Often we're not really choosing, but simply reacting or following old, ingrained patterns.

---

15 *The Light Shall Set You Free*

The goal is to raise our vibrational frequency and to keep it as positive and as high as possible. But if we're not paying attention—if we're simply reacting or running on autopilot—it's easy for other people's negative attitudes to penetrate our thoughts or feelings. Since everything vibrates, vibrations from other people and from places and things are all around us, affecting us without our being aware. We may know something is wrong, but we haven't made the connection between cause and effect. We're affected by what we read or hear through the media (TV, radio, internet) and even by excessive noise, machinery, and equipment. According to Abraham[16], we are always getting a perfect vibrational match to whatever we are predominantly *giving our attention to.*

Although we can choose what we let in and what we keep out, we don't always exercise our freedom of choice. Often we're like sieves, indiscriminately letting anything and everything affect us. We have to develop the habit of noticing what's going on around us and how it's affecting us before we can decide what to pay attention to and what to avoid.

While it's obviously a good idea to limit our exposure to negative people, situations, and things that drain our energy, most of us also have some attitudes and behaviors that lower our own vibrational frequency, as well as the vibrational frequencies of those we come in contact with. Some of those attitudes and behaviors, which we may not even be consciously aware of, are:

- not taking care of ourselves to the point of becoming worn down or even sick

- getting overinvolved in other people's problems

---

[16] Abraham is a non-physical group consciousness with whom Esther Hicks has been communicating since 1985. The collection of published books based on the information she has received is referred to as the Teachings of Abraham.

- consistently over-working or over-doing so that we forget to protect ourselves

- getting sucked into negative feelings and staying there

- being in destructive relationships

- letting things slide or being irresponsible

- living in the past or in the future instead of in the moment

- taking on other people's negative attitudes

- constantly criticizing ourselves or others or being around critical people

- addictions or obsessions of any type (eating, shopping, alcohol, drugs, etc.)

- negative emotions: anger, fear, resentment, depression, shame, guilt, jealousy, greed, etc.

Negative thinking lowers our vibration, weakens our auric shield, and leaves us unprotected. It closes us down to love and to the flow of abundance, and it prevents us from seeing the positive in the world around us. Negative thinking attracts more negativity, and that's what can get us stuck. Not only can negative thinking make you ill, your negative thoughts can develop into negative thought forms, which become entity-like over time.

I don't have the ability to raise someone else's vibrational frequency because I can't think and feel for anyone else. But the guides can do it on a temporary basis. Jesus can do it, too, which is one of the reasons he stays in people after they've had a healing session, sometimes for as long as four days. I've noticed people's vibrational frequency lift as a result of a healing session, but it doesn't stay at that level all by itself. It's up to each of us to learn to assess how we feel, so we can then choose positive thoughts, behaviors, and attitudes that raise our own vibrational frequency. Some of the things we can do to raise our vibration are:

- meditating on a regular basis, even for 15 minutes a day[17]

- using positive affirmations and visualizations

- staying in communication with our guides—*but only those who are here for our highest and best good*—and especially with the Arcturians

- tapping into the higher vibration of these multi-dimensional beings (Arcturians, Ascended Masters, Star Beings, archangels, and angels)

- focusing on love, the highest vibration of all

- learning how to be mindful and aware instead of asleep

- learning how to redirect negative thoughts

- releasing negative emotions; letting go of the past

- forgiving ourselves

- forgiving those who we feel have wronged us

- asking for help when we need it, instead of sinking deeper and deeper into despair

- tuning out the critical inner voice

- being active instead of passive; changing the things in our lives that don't work

Changing Negative Patterns

Of course, the older we are, the harder it can be to change ingrained patterns of thinking. But I can attest to the fact that it's never too late—not that I'm that old. It isn't easy, and it isn't a project you complete and put aside, never to return to. Learning to change

---

[17] Regular meditation is an extremely important practice. A great tool for beginners is *Getting into the Vortex: Guided Meditation CD and User Guide* by Esther and Jerry Hicks.

negative patterns is an ongoing process. But once you begin doing it and have success with it, it does get easier. You become more aware of what doesn't work. You examine your beliefs instead of accepting them automatically.

A belief is just a thought you continue thinking. We were taught things in childhood that we may never have reconsidered or reasoned out for ourselves, things that may or may not be accurate. We aren't even aware of some of the beliefs we have, yet even those beliefs can affect us and alter our vibrational frequency. The book *The Law of Attraction* can help you focus on your belief systems so that you can take a look at which of your beliefs are not serving you and are not for your highest and best good.

Once you realize you have the ability to change negative beliefs and change the things that don't work, you can take the steps to free yourself from them. You can begin to attract and create positive thoughts, beliefs, and feelings that are for your highest and best good and that raise your vibrational frequency and strengthen your auric shield.

Identify What Doesn't Work

If you already know which things in your life lower your vibrational frequency, you're at a good starting point. If you aren't sure, then the first thing to do is to begin paying attention to how people and situations—or even your own thoughts and actions—affect you. One way to do that is to keep a journal and at the end of each day write down what happened during the day and how you felt. Over time, you'll begin to see patterns, and soon you'll be able to notice your reactions in the moment, as you are having them.

Choose to Change

Maybe you have a very good idea of what things in your life aren't working, but you're used to the way things are, or you're afraid you can't do anything about them. Or maybe you've just started discovering some negative patterns. In either case, the next thing to do is recognize that you now have a choice about what you attract and create in your life, and then choose to begin manifesting those things that raise your vibrational frequency.

Decide How to Go About It

There are many proven tools and techniques already out there that you can use to learn how to accentuate the positive, as the old song says. You attract whatever you give your attention to, so instead of focusing on what you don't want (or want less of), focus on what you do want or what you want more of. Some tools I've used are the books, CDs, and tapes by Esther and Jerry Hicks, especially their book *The Law of Attraction*, and books by Louise Hay, including *You Can Heal Your Life*. Find something you resonate with, something you can begin using right now.

Do It!

No book or CD or class is magic all by itself. None of them can do the work for you. Once you make a commitment to changing something, you have to follow through by doing the work to transform the negative into something positive. The good news and the bad news is that you're the only one who can do it. And wherever you set your foot down on the path, wherever you begin, it will lead you to the next step and the next step and the step after that. Following a spiritual path means focusing on the journey, one step at a time, not on the destination.

Making Good Vibrational Choices

My own first step on the path was reading *The Secret* by Rhonda Byrne. I read through it once, quickly, and then read it again, more slowly, taking notes. I wrote down the quotes or affirmations that I felt raised my vibration. I still have the notebook, and I've continued adding to it from other things I've read. It's a very important part of my practice, and I try to keep up with it.

I can't do the healing work I do when I have a low vibration or I'm down. I can only do this work when my vibration is high, and even then I have to go into a meditative state ahead of time to prepare. So when I notice my vibrational frequency is low, I use those words and quotes from my notebook to help raise it. As Abraham says, when your vibrational frequency is low, it's usually because of your thinking. You've tapped into the negative energy on this third-dimensional planet so you're not feeling very good. One of the things I tell myself is that it's incredibly important that I'm feeling good and that my vibration is high. I want better feeling thoughts—thoughts that make me feel better. As soon as you tap into one of those thoughts, it will lead you to another and then another.

Our thoughts determine our feelings, and our feelings tell us what vibrational frequency we're on. Our minds are running constantly with thousands of thoughts a day. It's impossible to monitor each and every one of them. But if you monitor your feelings, they will tell you what your thoughts are. *Am I feeling good? Am I just feeling okay? Am I feeling bad?*

If you're feeling bad, ask yourself what you were just thinking, and you'll discover the cause of your feelings. If you shift your thinking to better-feeling thoughts—positive thoughts—you'll attract more of the same kinds of thoughts, which will raise your vibrational frequency and make you feel better. It actually helps to get in the habit of paying attention to how your thoughts make you feel regardless of whether it's good, bad, or just okay. Why bother to pay attention to your thoughts when you're feeling good? Our tendency is to simply accept feeling good, to pay no attention to our thoughts because there's no problem. But if we tune out the thoughts that make us feel good, then when there *is* a problem—when our vibration is low—we may have a harder time shifting our thinking to those better-feeling thoughts.

Some things we do may feel satisfying in the short-term. Repeatedly slacking off, using drugs, gambling, or engaging in any type of compulsive behavior may be momentarily gratifying but usually has negative consequences. Instead of raising our vibrational frequency, those kinds of activities actually lower it and weaken our auric shields. It's important to differentiate between things that make us feel good *and raise our vibrational frequency* and things that make us feel good for a short time but lower our vibrational frequency.

The situations and activities that raise one person's vibrational frequency may have a different effect on someone else. There is no one-size-fits-all list we could make of people, places, things, and situations that are positive and people, places, things, and situations that are negative. I could make a list for myself, but it wouldn't necessarily fit you, and vice versa. It isn't black and white. Each of us has to make those discoveries on our own, and in order to do that, we have to pay attention to how we feel. Instead of developing a belief or a concept of "good" situations and "bad" situations, we need to be mindful of how we're reacting to things and how they're affecting us. Does this person or situation have a positive effect or a negative effect on me? When I'm engaged in this activity, do I feel good or do I feel bad?

First Things First

Before you can succeed at raising your vibrational frequency to the highest level, you need to have all entities—Reptilians, demons, and discarnates—and all cords and attachments removed. If you still have any of these things in or around you, it will be much harder, if not impossible, for you to keep your vibrational frequency up. All these entities, especially Reptilians, are very good at getting you to look the other way. They don't want you to raise your vibrational frequency, and they will do everything in their power to block you from doing it.

Protecting Yourself

You can't always avoid negative people, places, and situations, and you can't exert direct control over other people's thoughts, feelings, or behaviors. That's where protection comes into the picture. Just as raising your vibrational frequency isn't something you do once and never again, protecting yourself is also something to be mindful of and practice on a regular basis. It's a moment-by-moment practice. It requires effort and attention, and we like to be lazy—myself included. I'd like to not have to do anything. But protection doesn't work that way.

Even if you're protecting yourself on a regular basis, you may occasionally find yourself heading into a potentially negative or difficult situation. In that case, it's helpful to recognize what you're going into ahead of time and think about how you're going to handle it. Come up with a plan. Set your intention as to what you want to say or how you want to act. When I do that, things generally work out. When I go into one of those situations and don't think about it ahead of time, it doesn't take long for me to realize I forgot to protect myself or my vibration is going down.

You may already be doing something or have a practice to protect yourself that seems to work for you and makes you feel good. There are lots of different rituals people use to create sacred space or to cleanse and protect themselves. And people have been using objects or talismans for the purpose of protection for centuries. But protection doesn't come from the words or actions in a ritual or from any particular object or talisman. The purpose of rituals or talismans is to focus your thoughts and your attention and increase your receptiveness to positive, uplifting spiritual feelings—to make a connection with Source. How you do that is less important than that you do it with intention.

After enough repetition, anything you do for protection can become a routine you're no longer attentive to. If you recite a prayer or perform a ritual automatically without any awareness or intention behind it—simply going through the motion—there's not much power in it. What you're doing shouldn't be putting you to sleep; it should be waking you up. But if you use the words or the activity or the object in order to be mindful and awake, then it will lift your vibrational frequency. For example, a simple ritual at the end of the day is to list all the things you're grateful for. Doing something like that creates positive thoughts and feelings and raises your vibration.

We would begin saying, "I'm not ever going to get it done. I'm an eternally expanding Being, and I'm doing great where I am, and I'm so eager about what's coming." That's the essence of the vibration that keeps adventurous things coming, keeps you feeling always excited, stable and secure, keeps you feeling in love with life. All day, every day, count your blessings! All day, every day, make your lists of things you appreciate. And as you keep activating what is working in your life, then more pleasing things on all subjects will flow to you.

Abraham[18]

---

[18] Abraham-Hicks Publications; excerpted from the workshop in North Los Angeles, CA on Saturday, March 6th, 2004 #648

Keeping your vibrational frequency high helps strengthen your auric shield, which will protect you from absorbing the negative vibrations of others and from other entities (demons and discarnates) as well as cords and attachments. I usually don't see auras in the course of my work, but I often see people's light. Sometimes when I'm first working with someone who has Reptilians or demons, I see no light in them at all. But when I scan again after the entities have been removed, I suddenly do see a light. The light may be small, but it's growing. Our auric shields respond the same way. When we're up at the high end of the emotional continuum—at the loving, happy, blissful stage—then our auric shields are strong. They're wide. They're healthy. The negativity can't penetrate them. But when we're down at the low end of the continuum, we're vulnerable to all kinds of negativity.

We're responsible for maintaining our own auric shields. No healer or anyone else can substantially affect your auric shield or maintain it. That's our work, yours and mine, as individuals.

Raising our vibrational frequency is absolutely the best thing we can do to protect ourselves. It's something we need to do every day, every hour, every minute. It can be challenging, especially when we're getting bombarded with negativity on a daily basis. It's challenging for me, and I fail at it on a regular basis. But I do my best to recognize when I've failed and pull myself back up by doing what I can to raise my vibration.

What you do is miniscule in comparison with what you choose to think, because your vibration is so much more powerful and so much more important.

Abraham[19]

---

[19] Abraham-Hicks Publications; excerpted from the workshop in Boston, MA on Sunday, October 20th, 1996 #268

In my experience, working at keeping my vibrational frequency high is better protection than any ritual or practice or object. But if performing a particular ritual or practice or using a special object keeps you mindful and raises your vibration, then by all means continue with it.

Please remember, however, that if you have any entities or cords or attachments, no ritual or talisman will protect you. If you have anything in you, you will have a very difficult time keeping other entities, attachments, or cords out because then you'll have a battle going on on two fronts. Not only will you be battling yourself and the negativity that's permeating you from society and your environment, you will also be battling major negativity inside you that's trying to keep you down and further weaken your auric shield. It's extremely challenging, to put it mildly, to keep your vibration up or protect yourself when you still have entities in you.

And any rituals you perform will have **no effect whatsoever** on any Reptilians that may be in you or around you. All entities need to be removed first; *then* you can work on protecting yourself without expending extra energy fending off their influence. The Arcturians are the greatest—really the only—protection against Reptilians. If you want to be protected against Reptilians, the Arcturians invite you to connect with them and call on them regularly. Get to know the guides who are here for your highest and best good and call on them as often as you need to. They are also here to help protect you.

All three people in the next chapter who have been doing this work with me have their own methods of protecting themselves. But they all work on keeping their vibrational frequencies high, and when it comes to the Reptilians, they all call on the Arcturians for protection.

Chapter 13
Healing Planet Earth

Is This Work for You?

Some of you who are reading this book will intuitively know you can do this work—that you've been called to do it. Others may be thinking, "Well, this sounds simple. I'll just call in the Arcturians, and then I'll start removing Reptilians." But, as you'll read in this chapter, it is far from that simple or that easy. You have to have the right intention. You need to prepare yourself so you're ready for it. Your vibration has to be high. And you need to make sure you're protected. Most importantly, you have to be connected to the Arcturians and accept their download.

The fact is that you and I cannot do this at all. A human being does not have the power to remove Reptilians. If we did, this planet would be an entirely different place already. We are necessary in order for the work to be done, but it's the Arcturians, not us, who remove Reptilians.

Yes, I'd like to see a thousand, ten thousand, a million people out there around the planet who are connected with the Arcturians and doing this work, so I'm certainly not trying to scare everyone away.

But at the same time, I want those who are reading this to be aware it is not child's play. It's not for everyone. This work is serious *spiritual warfare* and you need to take it seriously. These Reptilians are powerful—not as powerful as the Arcturians, but they're very dangerous. If you decide to engage them, be aware you'll be painting a bull's eye on your chest.

Lisa and Robert, who were the other two-thirds of the healing team working with Carl at the time we first encountered the Reptilians, know all of this first-hand. So does Ellen, who I've been training, and who has been doing this work, too. I asked each of them to tell me what it's been like for them to do the work and what advice they have for anyone else who wants to begin doing it.

They've all experienced the downside. The work can be extremely difficult, and it can take a toll on you if you're not scrupulous about keeping your vibration high. But they've experienced the upside, too, which comes not only from removing Reptilians, but also from developing a personal connection with the very powerful, very loving Arcturians. All of us have found connecting with the Arcturians to be uplifting and beneficial.

Of course, we're all still learning. We may be at different stages in the learning process, and each person progresses at a different pace, but I don't think the process ever ends. There is always more to discover, more that will be revealed to us once we're ready to receive it.

Lisa: *Opening a New Gateway*

Before the work we did with Carl, I wasn't aware of the Reptilian presence on our planet, around our planet, and controlling us. I wasn't aware there were dark forces trying to control us or hurt us or feed off of us. I thought everything was love and light, love and light.

During our sessions with Carl, Lisa, who is a healer and a gifted psychic, acted as the intermediary between the rest of us and the three "guests" who managed to string us along in the beginning. She was the person directly communicating with them. As soon as they realized we were on to the fact they were Reptilians, they attacked her and tried to get her to throw herself across the room.

So learning about the Reptilians was hardly fun for her. But at the same time, connecting with the Arcturians has opened a new gateway for the work she does. And the knowledge she's gained from these healing sessions and events has helped her see what is often really holding people back from experiencing the love and light.

Tuning in to the Arcturians two years ago has taken my work as a healer and psychic to another level and transformed my knowingness of the universe. Before my experience with Carl, I was only aware of the angelic realm and the Masters, like Jesus. I wasn't really aware of the celestial beings, our brothers and sisters of the stars. Being introduced to the Arcturians has definitely taken my work in a different direction.

It is our birthright to emanate radiance, but because of the Reptilian presence on our Earth, many people are not capable of ascending or acknowledging their birthright, which is being a radiant being of light.

It's nice to know there are beings of light out there who love and want to assist humanity in breaking free of the falsehoods the Reptilians have perpetuated on us for thousands and thousands of years.

I often refer people to Lisa after my work with them is finished. Whether she works with them one time or on an ongoing basis, she often has a better sense of the difference it can make when people have these entities, especially the Reptilians, removed.

The people I work with afterward are amazed at how life has become a more positive experience, rather than a negative one. They can actually feel and sense and love again instead of being angry and grumpy and blaming the world for their troubles. They realize they were walking in a lot of fear because that's what the Reptilians feed off of. Now they are capable of experiencing higher vibrational love, happiness, and joy.

Usually they come to me wanting to know their soul's purpose and to get on their soul's path. They're able and ready to acknowledge they have a spiritual path, and they want to assist humanity. They don't want a life that's about service to self: me, me, me; stuff, stuff, stuff; get, get, get. They really want to assist others in finding that love and light and happiness.

Everyone who worked with Carl wishes he'd been able to have that kind of an experience, too. That's what all of us on the healing team were hoping for when we got together. But he hasn't had the dramatic change or positive results so many others have had.

Carl definitely has some karmic issues to deal with and some psychic wounds that I don't think we worked on. And although the Reptilians were removed, it appears he can still be manipulated and controlled by the frequencies they continue to broadcast.

Working With the Light

Lisa now calls on the Arcturians in most of her sessions, whether or not she's removing Reptilians. She practices what she calls light therapy, in which she uses the light—either orbs of light or shafts of light—the Arcturians are able to send into her clients for protection and for healing.

This is what she sees when the Arcturians use light to remove Reptilians.

A shaft of light sent from the Arcturians enters the client from the top of the head and then travels down the spine all the way out through the pelvis area, connecting the person to Gaia and grounding him or her. Then the shaft of light starts vibrating at a high frequency. When it starts vibrating, it also starts expanding, and within the shaft of light a vortex is created. If you were to look down into the shaft of light from the top, you would see it start spinning. It looks kind of like a tornado, spinning and spinning and spinning. The Reptilians are swept up within the shaft of light that becomes a vortex, and they are lifted up and out into a spacecraft.

The shaft of light is like a tunnel and it connects above to an even larger tunnel of light. When I look up to see what's beyond the light, sometimes I can see a spacecraft.

Her impression is that not all of the Reptilians are taken to a spacecraft. The ones who are removed from inside people or around people are usually just sent to the Light.

If there's a Reptilian outside someone or outside the auric field harassing someone, usually two or three Arcturians will come down and surround the Reptilian. Sometimes they put a net of light around it and take it up to the Light. Sometimes they stun it and a couple of Arcturians carry it up to the Light.

The Reptilians don't put up much of a fight when they're caught. I think the vibrational frequency is too high for them, and they can't handle it. It doesn't kill them, but it stuns them. Once they're immobilized, they can be safely taken to the Light.

I have never seen the Reptilians being taken to an Arcturian spacecraft as Lisa has. However, the Reptilians are very hierarchical, with the Draconians at the highest level. They're more protected by the Reptilian troops and harder to get since they're usually down in the underground bases. It's the Draconians, who, once captured by the Arcturians, are the most likely Reptilians to be taken up to a spacecraft. What happens to them there, I don't know.

Lisa hasn't encountered very many Draconians. She says they are elusive and much more intelligent than the other Reptilians, who she describes as having a thug mentality and relying on brute force.

I find the Draconians extremely difficult to remove. I call upon a lot of Arcturians when I'm face-to-face with a Draconian.

She has gotten stronger in the course of the two years since we first encountered the Reptilians.

The first year or even year and a half was more challenging. But the more I connect with the Arcturians, and the more I continue to facilitate this work, the easier it becomes. It's not my favorite thing to do, but I do it. I don't have to see the Reptilians' faces anymore (which helps). I just know by their frequency what we're dealing with.

At the beginning, the Reptilians definitely did not want me to work with the Arcturians or continue in this line of work. So they set up obstacles and influenced others to try to stop my connection and the work. But I've prevailed.

Staying Connected With the Arcturians

Lisa has developed relationships with several Arcturians and feels the presence of a council of 12 around her at all times. Not only do they support and guide her, they also help her access her higher self and remain in the Light, and they protect her as she navigates through the day-to-day aspects of our third-dimensional world.

I don't actually see them, but she does.

When they make their entrance, they're these light beings I see from afar with my third eye, coming closer and closer until I can see eyes and what looks like a slit for a nose and a slit for a mouth. They don't have human-looking faces. They generally first appear as colors and orbs, oval orbs, like oval beings of light. The color of the light varies from violet to blue, depending on which group is coming to speak with me. My council of 12 is blue, but others I channel or who assist me sometimes radiate violet.

Sometimes they are small beings of light, maybe about four feet tall. But depending on what they're assisting with, they can expand and become very tall, up to ten or twelve feet. They're especially likely to do that when I'm going into a very dense place with a lot of Reptilian-controlled beings.

I don't see lower legs or feet; I see gowns. They are more light than physical form. They're translucent, so although they have shape, they don't have the dense flesh or the form that we have.

Offering Guidance for Others

Lisa has been doing this work about as long as I have, so she has a lot of experience and some excellent—and crucial—advice for anyone who thinks they want to start removing Reptilians.

The most important thing is that your vibrational frequency has to be high enough. The Arcturians have laid it out for us. There are universal laws that have been given to us through other channels, which are guidelines for us to function at a high frequency. It's important that we not only know these universal laws, but that we also truly practice them. It's about walking your talk and trying to be as pure as possible.

You have to really know Spirit and feel Spirit within every cell of your body. You have to have a devotional discipline in order to connect with the Arcturians and connect with your other spiritual families.

And I think you also have to be sure you're unplugged from the mass consciousness. Have the discipline to not watch television or read the news. Have the discipline to maybe not even go to the movies or listen to popular music. Have the discipline to know what is yours and what is not yours.

Basically, I feel that anyone doing this needs to be pure in a vibrational, emotional, and spiritual sense, because the Reptilians will use anything to hurt or control you—particularly if you're going to engage in removing them. If you want to confront these dark, powerful forces, you need to be at a high frequency and pure. If you have a negative thought-stream forming within your brain, the Reptilians can manipulate it and expand it so that it fills every part of your body.

The Reptilians know what your weaknesses are, and those are the places where they will attack you. They know how to push your buttons. If you have any insecurities, they'll amplify them. They'll push you toward whatever causes you to slip and fall. If you have any kind of addiction you're trying to work on or recover from, they will do whatever they can to keep you addicted. They will use anything that causes your vibration to drop. Maybe you're out driving and someone cuts you off and you get angry. That lowers your vibration. That's an example of the simple kinds of thing they will use.

You have to do the work to remain positive and loving and to really know who you are and what your mission is. Otherwise, you're likely to be kicked around and used and abused.

If we're not pure of heart and filled with Light, the Reptilians can infiltrate us and manipulate us very easily with their dense frequencies, which come in many forms and are constantly bombarding us. They play games with people who think they're doing removals. You may think you're working with the Arcturians and helping people, but you'll actually be planting seeds in people. So you have to have a high vibration or you'll end up unconsciously working for the Reptilians.

Unless you feel divinely inspired to do this work and be connected with the Arcturians, you shouldn't attempt it.

It has to be divinely inspired because if you're trying to do it for your ego and calling attention to yourself—*Look at me! Look at me! I can remove Reptilians! I'm so amazing!*—then you're going to have an interesting experience, and it won't be a positive one. The Reptilians will go after your ego. The work definitely has to come from your heart.

Facing Her Challenges

The Reptilians want to control everyone, and they always go after the weak link in the chain. If they can't get to you directly, they will go around you and try to get to someone who is close to you. As Lisa said, they are extremely adept at manipulating people.

The Reptilians have a very low, dense vibration, lower than ours. There's a complete imbalance within them. They have hearts that beat, but they have no idea about the vibration of love. Everything for them is the extreme. The only emotions they know are fear-based, which is the opposite of love. So as far as their spiritual development is concerned, they are way down the vibrational line. Human beings experience fear, but we can also experience love. We can experience the connection with the Creator of All That Is. We can also radiate love that heals and touches others.

What the Reptilians have over us is their technology, and they use their technological powers to manipulate the human species. When they first came to the Earth plane, they gave humans agriculture. They gave them technologies to help them with building. Humanity took great leaps in social organization. So the Reptilians were seen as gods, even though they are lower on the spiritual evolution scale, because they were technologically advanced.

Several months ago, a client of Lisa's who works in the Boston area told her she had been feeling something underneath her feet. Lisa called on the Arcturians to assist her, and they showed her that the Reptilians had an underground base in that location.

The Arcturians sent orbs of light down into the portal, and we saw all these passageways, all these Reptilians, and they actually had computers and screens and desks. It looked like an office set up, but the Arcturians told me it was a manipulation control center. The orbs of white light stunned the Reptilians who were down there, and the Arcturians started removing them with shafts of light.

The shafts of light just started spinning, and the Reptilians and the furniture and the computers got swept up into this vortex of white light that lifted everything up and out and into the spacecraft above.

The Arcturians almost never leave a portal or tunnel or base open. First they make sure everything is removed and all the Reptilians are gone, then they energetically close the portal so it can't be used again. Lisa saw the Arcturians put a protective covering of light over the opening of that underground facility. Two or three days later, she learned from another source that a number of the Reptilians' underground bases in that area had been taken out.

Lisa's Message From the Arcturians

The Arcturians communicated this message for us through Lisa:

Greetings, beloved brothers and sisters on the Earth plane. We are most grateful for the abilities of the humans on the Earth plane to connect with higher vibrational celestial beings. We have been waiting for this time to be able to serve humanity and those who want to lift their frequency and embody more of the light. Indeed, there are beings who do not serve for love and light, but in fact serve for the opposite, fear and control. However, many on the Earth plane are awakening to the deception and lies that have been perpetuated upon your planet for millennia.

Now we are able to offer our support in large numbers. In past times, we were not able to assist due to the free will that is a universal law that we follow directly. The time to reunite with the celestial beings who watch over the Earth is coming soon. There are more individuals who are willing to communicate with the brothers and sisters of the stars and who are able to lift their frequency to perform such a feat.

We will continue to guide and support those who ask for our assistance. We are filled with wisdom that will assist those on their spiritual journey to reach higher and higher states of love and being. We are so grateful for those who have opened up their third eyes and their crowns in addition to their heart centers and who have taken that leap of faith to connect with us and our abilities to assist the Earth in breaking free from the prison she has been suppressed within for thousands and thousands of years.

Robert: *Healing the Whole Planet*

Is it important to keep a high vibration? Is it important for us to do this work? Yes, it is. Unfortunately, I don't think the mainstream really understands yet that everything is energy. All of our laws of physics, as we know them, are being challenged, and our perception of the world is being challenged. And I would suggest that you and I, Wayne, are working on the edges of this.

Robert, a channeler and a healer I met in a channeling workshop, is very knowledgeable about many aspects of the spiritual realms. But what really stands out about him is that he doesn't back down from anything. When something does manage to knock him down, he gets back up and keeps going.

The work Robert and I have done together isn't the type of work he ordinarily does. But he was a powerful presence on the healing team, and he's since worked with a few others like Carl who have had Reptilians from an early age or even from birth.

We can clear some people of everything, but because they have been conditioned, they fall back into a mindset of victimhood. Not everybody I've worked with has done that, but certainly those who have it from an early age find it very hard to progress. It's not as if everything is lost if someone has been controlled since birth. But there are different degrees to which we can expect people to heal if they've been under the Reptilians' control for most of their lives.

So much depends on the individual keeping a high vibrational frequency and doing his or her own work after being cleared. As Robert said, it isn't up to the Arcturians or Jesus or anyone else to do that. They *can't* do it. Each person has to do it for him or herself.

Even when you clear not just people, but places, it isn't always permanent. I believe it is the individual's responsibility, ultimately, to maintain the space. And I don't mean just their own personal space; I mean the wider area, the space in which they live.

If you aren't keeping your vibration high and your auric shield becomes weakened, it's all too easy for demons, discarnates, attachments, and cords to get their hooks into you. This is doubly the case if you've had entities, especially Reptilians, for years or even decades.

Remember that these entities can affect you subtly at first. You may not notice them right away, which is exactly the way they want it. And once they get back into you, they manipulate your thinking.

That makes it very, very difficult to persuade someone that there's a problem, even though you or I can see that there's a vast difference in his or her behavior and energy. It's always projected onto something or someone else.

Robert has experience working with, and on, other light workers, with whom he's had success.

There's a distinction between those who have had these entities all their lives so it's difficult for them to make very much headway and those who, because they are on a path of light, are already seeking and searching and preparing themselves to raise their vibration.

We all create our own reality, and that's one of the hard things that we, as light workers, have to cope with.

Experiencing the Arcturians

Each of us who has worked with the Arcturians has our own personal experience of them, but some things—their subtlety, their high vibrational frequency, their lovingness, and their power—are felt by all of us.

They are very different from angelic energies. And they always come, for me, as a group consciousness. I don't see an individual Arcturian or a light or anything. I just sense them. And they don't seem to have a personality. Archangel Michael, on the other hand, has a very strong personality, not egoistically, but energetically. But the Arcturian force is very humble, yet powerful. And they're very quick and very effective in what they do. If they can't shift something, then I know we've got a real issue because I know how potent their energy is.

Robert told me he doesn't call on the Arcturians a lot, but tends to hold them in reserve.

They are not a panacea. They're not a silver bullet. However, when I do need to bring out the big guns, and I ask them to sweep through something, they're incredibly effective. I can feel a shift in energy immediately.

I'm wondering if I should be using them more frequently in some of the work I do, and if I should dig a little deeper when I do my consultation before a reading. That's something I'm still learning about—when and how to use the Arcturians.

Focusing on the Bigger Picture

Both Robert and I—as well as many other people—have been involved in larger-scale healings, not just locally, but in different places throughout the world.

There is a wider context of not just healing ourselves as individuals, but also healing the Earth itself because it contains portals and embedded souls, discarnates, whatever you want to call them. All of this work is helping to raise the frequency. And the Arcturians are involved very closely in that. They have a particular affinity for working not just with people, but with location, which brings us to Gaia and the bigger picture of healing the planet.

Quite often souls are trapped here and can't find their way to the Light. They get stuck in the earth itself or in someone's aura because they've seen it as a light. As more and more of them come, there's a downward spiral. The energy of an area becomes very low and negative. I can feel that. Some would say it sends chills down your spine.

Often when we're doing work to help souls pass over, I use angels and help them to open portals of light for the souls that have been stuck to pass through. But inevitably at the end of it, I ask the Arcturians for a cleansing, which I see as spirals of light that sweep upward through an individual. And as the Arcturians do that, they carry away any residue up into the Light. So they work in a very complementary fashion, as well as on their own.

When he works with his clients, he uses light in a manner similar to the way Lisa uses it.

The main part of my work is the releasing of energies and then showing people how to maintain that state. I work primarily with the angelic frequencies, drawing pure white angelic light all the way down through the person's crown chakra and out of the soles of the feet, making sure it goes down into the earth itself. A lot of the clients I work with do not have their energy fully in their bodies, often because they have pushed the energy down into the lower chakras or the lower part of the body, which often manifests in physical problems. They may only be inhabiting—energetically—the top half or top two thirds of the body, or even worse, they may not be in their body at all, which is what we call being spaced out or blissed out.

Bringing pure white light down and making sure it grounds is vital. So is asking for angelic protection by creating a circle of light around us in order to create a boundary, a clear space within which we can say we're going to lift our vibration. We're not trying to lift the entire neighborhood. We're just making sure our own personal space is clear and kept at a good, clean, high vibrational state.

Maintaining Good Housekeeping

Robert echoes what I talked about in the previous chapter on protection. In order to stay protected, we need to keep our vibrational frequency high and our auric shields strong. It's not something you can do once or even occasionally whenever you can fit it into your schedule. It's only effective if it becomes a daily practice.

As there is a greater awakening and understanding, I think people will start to realize that in the same way they wash their clothes and their bodies, they need to wash or cleanse their auras. And they need to do the same thing with their locations or physical possessions because each one carries a level of energy, particularly anything electrical, like computer systems or phones. It behooves us to have good housekeeping and to make sure everything is lifted and that we have a regular routine of infusing something with light. And then we need to maintain it.

Robert's Message From the Arcturians

Although Robert doesn't usually channel the Arcturians, he connected with them in order to receive a message for this book:

Indeed, we are here, for we have been here from the outset of humanity's mission on Earth. We are the guardians in the wings. And we come now with a message that we are here in these times of great change to assist in that role of guardian, but we will always take a back seat. We will not interfere with your free will. And we welcome the opportunity for you, Wayne, to broadcast to many that we are here, for unless we are called upon, we will not intrude.

For those who ask for our presence, we come willingly, and always in accordance with those themes you have outlined of healing, of lifting frequency, of releasing that which is stuck—in other words, of moving everything forward in a direction that lifts vibration and frequency and assists in the ascension of the planet and all on it.

These are those times of change. This is why we come to the fore now. We do not seek the limelight in an egotistical sense. We simply seek acknowledgement from others that we exist and that we are here to be of service and willingly so.

Much has been written about where we live and what our role is within the wider universe. But perhaps more pertinent to this time is that we are here to assist each individual. We are here to assist whenever you who may listen to this or may read these words feel that you need help to lift your mood or help to lift frequencies or energies that are not yours but have somehow become stuck within your auric field or your light body.

And of course we will do this, for that is how we grow through service, and it is our pleasure and joy to assist wherever possible. In this sense, we are akin in many ways to the angelic realms, but our vibration is different. We have gone through the process of being physical. We understand from our own history what it is like to work with dense physical vibrations, and so this is why we are here.

We are your older brothers, come from the stars to assist you in these times of great change.

Ellen: *Finding a Purpose in Life*

This seems to be my mission. I don't really get it, but it's like a calling or something. You get led into things, and at first you think you're just doing it as a hobby or out of curiosity, but then it turns into something else.

Ellen was actually at the Whole Foods store the day Lisa and I ran into Carl before the healing team began working with him. When I was gathering people together, I asked Ellen to be part of the team, but she knew herself well enough to realize she wasn't ready yet. And she was probably right. But I think after she saw that the rest of us were surviving the experience and progressing on our paths, she decided to jump in—with both feet, as it turned out.

That was actually encouraging to me since before Ellen came along, I wasn't sure whether this was something that could be taught to others. Now I know that, yes, it can be taught.

When I first met Ellen about three years ago, she had been going through a particularly difficult period in her life.

I had been on the spiritual path for a long time. I was a medium and did a lot of work on people and was very active in the spir-

itual world. Then when my husband passed away suddenly, I became really depressed and changed into a different person. Everything was dark. I had no interest in life. I lost all my passion, even for the spiritual work.

Although she was struggling, she had not given up. She told me later that she had been interested in the work I was doing right from the beginning, but whenever she thought about coming to see me, something would deter her—which, of course, is not uncommon. It's so hard for people to come to me when they have entities that are blocking them from doing so. She did attend one of the group sessions I held, and then she came back afterward for some individual healing work.

During one of those healing sessions, I discovered the Reptilians had placed an etheric implant in her jaw.

My jaw had been killing me for about five years. The Reptilians had put an implant in it in order to block my third eye and my crown chakra, but once the implant was removed, everything changed. I started to care about my life again, and about getting out and exercising and doing things.

Before the implant was removed, whenever anybody talked about aliens, my mind always said, "Oh, that's crazy." It doesn't say that anymore. The Reptilians were blocking me because they didn't want me to believe it.

Taking It to the Next Level

Most of the people I work with are grateful and relieved to have whatever was in them or blocking them removed, and when our healing sessions are finished, they go off and live their lives. I don't usually have any further contact with them. That definitely wasn't the case with Ellen.

I became really intrigued with wanting to help everybody else in the universe, so I started coming to you to learn. I thought I was just going to be there, and you would be doing the work, not me. But then I started participating, and you kind of led me into it.

It was easy. I began to feel what you felt, and then I learned from you how to create a vortex and send the entities to the Light. Before long, I thought I had to clear up everybody.

She laughs when she says she wanted to help clear everyone in the universe, but it was true. She began working on her immediate family members first and then branched out to other family members, friends, and even friends of friends. That's a pretty normal progression. It's the reason most of the healings I do, maybe 90% of removals, are on someone's family members and friends who aren't initially aware it's taking place.

People have said to me, "You can't clear this person or you can't clear that person because you're going against their free will." But something inside of me always told me it isn't free will to have those entities inside of you. God wouldn't want you to be attacked by those things. So I just keep clearing people at a distance.

It bears repeating again and again that the soul doesn't deny permission for this work. When you're asking for permission, and you hear "no," that's coming from the Reptilians. They won't let you penetrate through to the soul. The Reptilians are trying to maintain control, and they are not going to give you permission to remove them. That's why you need the Arcturians to send down their shaft of light to penetrate that veil or force field the Reptilians put up.

Ellen also brought several of her family members in to see me for individual sessions.

I intuitively knew way ahead of time that these entities try to prevent people from coming. And I would get so nervous whenever I had to bring somebody to your place, because I was afraid I wouldn't be able to get them there.

One of the first people Ellen brought to see me was her former daughter-in-law Cathy, with whom she'd maintained a close relationship. Cathy had an entity that was causing her problems with her back. According to Ellen, Cathy had not been open to being in a relationship, but a few days after the healing session when I removed the entity, Cathy went on a date and met the man she's now married to. He has a son and a daughter from a previous marriage, and Cathy knew right away there was something going on with the son. He'd been in trouble quite a bit and had a history of violent behavior. So Ellen and Cathy brought Cathy's new family in for a session, during which we removed some demons from Cathy's stepson.

That was the first session Ellen participated in with me. When I asked her if I could share some of her experiences for this book, she told me she rarely has an opportunity to talk to people about this, so she was happy to be able to talk about it with me. There is still a stigma attached to the subject of entities in general and specifically Reptilians. But I notice that more and more people are openly discussing it. David Icke has been writing and talking about it for nearly 20 years. When he first started speaking about it in public, he had maybe five people show up, now he has thousands come to his lectures. So the world is becoming aware of it.

Tuning in to the Energy

Throughout the time Ellen has been doing this work with me, she's faced her share of challenges. After the first healing session we were involved in together, she was so exhausted she felt as if she'd been hit by a train. She couldn't get out of bed the next day and was tired for the following two days, as well.

Although I didn't really understand it at the time, I knew it must have been an energetic thing. I thought, "Well, I guess that's part of it." I knew I would feel things in my body. When we tuned in to the energy, whatever the person [we were working on] had, I would feel it in my body. And then I would feel it leave. What I didn't realize is that it takes a certain amount of your own energy to do this.

I don't fully understand it, either, but in the course of these healings we are working and connecting with multidimensional beings—Ascended Masters, Star Beings, angels, etc.—who have a very high vibration. In order to tap into that high vibration, we have to raise our own vibrations higher. When I began doing healings, it used to wipe me out, too, and take me a couple of days to recover. The energies are very high, and they affect people differently.

Ellen's exhaustion didn't faze her for long, though. If anything, she tried to do too much, too soon. Sometimes people get overly enthusiastic and jump right into it; then when they experience the consequences, they totally shut down. Eventually Ellen learned to proceed gradually, with baby steps, because she found out that if you take on too much, you're likely to get clobbered. She had to learn that lesson. Each person has to go through his or her own learning process and build a foundation just like I did.

Any time we move too quickly, we can miss things that are subtle but may be extremely important. You have to be patient while you're working, too. Don't just move on to clearing the next person. Wait a while and see if there's another wave coming, more work to be done.

You've got to check and re-check and double-check. This isn't a fast thing. You have to be there a while.

Patience, thoroughness, and vigilance: it helps to master all three if you're going to try to do this. These dark force entities are extremely manipulative, and their manipulation can be quite subtle.

When these things are inside you, they take over your thinking. They poison your mind and pump in negative stuff, so you can't even think to ask somebody to clear you.

This doesn't just happen to people who aren't aware of or who have no experience with entities and attachments. It can happen to people who know all about them. The entities don't usually come in like a load of bricks dropped on your head. If they did come in that way, you would notice it pretty quickly, and you would do something about it. But often they come in very subtly and start working their negative energy on you. It can be hard to pick up on what's happening. They block you from Source, from connecting, from meditating. They block you from your spiritual life, your physical life, and enjoyment, in general. As Ellen pointed out, they especially block you from being around people who can remove them from you.

Surviving the Challenges

Ellen's current husband had a lot of negative energy, those negative thoughts I've talked about that turn into negative thought forms, then crystallize and become entity-like. It took some time to chip away at that block of negativity, but since he'd had it for several decades, we didn't try to disintegrate it all at once. That would have been too traumatic for him. He'd also had Reptilians in him for a long time, and Ellen participated in removing them. She's seen a big difference in him since then.

He used to go through mood changes, up and down. All of a sudden, he would become real cold and emotionless. For a week at a time, he wouldn't talk to anybody; he couldn't get out of bed. If I talked about love, he would say, "I don't want love." Now I realize that was the Reptilians. They don't want love, so they were saying that.

Now if he has a mood swing, it doesn't last very long. And he's started to open up more and more.

That's very positive for both Ellen and her husband, in spite of the consequences she deals with.

Removing Reptilians doesn't take long, but the repercussions of doing it are really cruel. Since I started doing this, I've had constant stomach problems. They always attack me there.

Everyone has a weak spot, and Ellen's is her stomach. She said it felt as though some of the people we cleared were shooting poison arrows at her stomach. Sometimes when that happens, she thinks about not doing this work anymore.

I guess they try to weaken me by doing that, and sometimes it works temporarily. But I am who I am, and I'll probably never stop doing the work. I think eventually good things are going to happen.

She makes an effort to shield herself, but she's an empath. She feels other people's aches and pains and takes a lot on that she'd probably rather not take on. But that's just who she is.

As I indicated in the introduction to this chapter, when you do this work, you become a target, and Ellen has experienced that.

Not only do you become a target, but your family members become targets, and even my pet became a target. They tried to blind my dog. Luckily, she isn't totally blind. We caught it in time. I believe she had a healing from Archangel Michael and Raphael and Jesus. But they'll stop at nothing to attack you and the people around you.

If you do energy work, and somebody comes in who has something that you're not aware of, whatever they have can jump onto you. So you have to ask for all kinds of protection in your home and for the people in your home and that the people who come in don't bring anything in—or if they do, that it'll go to the Light.

If you're not doing this work and are not a threat to these entities and attachments, you might be able to get by with some lapses of attention. But when we are doing the work, these things are all around us, ready to come in at the slightest sign of weakness—as soon as our vibration gets down. The second we give them an opening, they're in, and once one gets in, it holds the door open for others. They want to neutralize us so we're no longer a threat to them, so we're no longer working for the Light. If they can do that, they've succeeded. And they have succeeded with a lot of people. That's why we need to keep our vibration up as much as possible.

If you're tired or sick, you should not do this at all. Before someone starts doing this work, they have to be clear, calm, centered, and ready for it. It's imperative they have a high vibration. Maybe those people [who are ready] will be guided to it. It's not child's play. It can be deadly.

Ellen has been connected with the Arcturians from her first healing session, and she has accepted their download.

I can feel their energy as they come in, and I talk to them. I haven't seen them, but they communicate with me telepathically. It's a soft kind of energy.

She continues to be challenged, but that's true for all of us.

I'm really glad to be of service and to help the planet because it feels like I have a purpose.

Chapter 14
Putting It All Into Practice

Do Your Own Work First

B eing cleared yourself can feel so good that it may be tempting to immediately try clearing other people, especially those closest to you. That's natural. You want them to feel as good as you do. But it's absolutely critical that you first focus on doing your own work and on learning how to keep your vibration up and your auric shield strong. By being consistent, you can build and maintain the solid foundation you'll need in order to do this work and not get beaten up all the time. Maintaining a regular practice—keeping up "good housekeeping"—can help you recover when you do get attacked.

And if you decide to undertake this work, make sure you have another spirit releasement practitioner available to scan you from time to time. It's easier to remove entities from someone else than it is to remove them from yourself.

We will never arrive at a point where we can relax and stop being vigilant, but I have found that the more I focus on keeping my vibration up and staying positive and clear, the easier it is to remember to do it. The healings themselves don't catch me off guard, anymore. It's when I stop paying attention minute-by-minute that I'm more likely to get attacked.

What Works for Me

Over time and through trial and error, I've learned what works for me before, during, and after a session. Consciously following these steps makes me more effective in the healing sessions and ensures my own protection and well-being.

Before

When I'm preparing myself to work on anyone—before I even see or talk to the person or go in from a distance—I make sure I'm clean and clear and my vibrational frequency is as high as possible. I also make sure the room I'm going to be working in is clean, as is the entire building. I meditate and call in the Arcturians and my guides for everyone's protection. I do all of that for my own benefit ahead of time because once I get started, I don't always have a lot of time. Usually, the demons begin engaging me immediately. They try to take me out because they know they're going to be gone, and they don't want to leave. So I have to be prepared to go to work in an instant.

Most of the time, I communicate with the person I'll be working on prior to the actual session so I have an idea ahead of time what I'm likely to find once we begin. When I scan the person beforehand, I let myself go in just a little bit, and if my arm twitches, that's Archangel Rafael letting me know something's there. I can tell instantly if there are demons, because demons make me nauseous. A pinch on the neck means there are Reptilians. I don't have to go in any deeper to know someone has demons and/or Reptilians.

People are not alike, and we don't all have the same abilities or sensitivities. Not everyone feels nauseous when demons are present. And although I don't see them, you may be able to if you have that particular gift. If you pay attention to your own reactions, you will learn how to sense them. It takes practice. But as far as the Reptilians are concerned, you always need the Arcturians to pierce the veil and remove the force field in order to detect them. That's the only way to be sure.

As soon as I identify the demons, they immediately start engaging me. So I'll ask Archangel Michael to block the transmission from them until the time is right to go in and do the removal. I'll also ask the Arcturians to do the same with the Reptilians.

When I'm working with someone who then asks me to check on another person, usually at a distance, I don't know ahead of time what to expect. I don't find out until the minute I scan that person.

When I say "scan," I don't mean visually. I do it by feeling or sensing. It's a kind of energetic analysis. Maybe a better way to put it is that it opens an energetic connection. I use it not only on people, but also on animals, homes, buildings, even objects. It used to take me a lot longer to go through the scanning process, and I wasn't always sure exactly what I was sensing. Now I get instant confirmation so I can tell if the person I'm scanning would benefit from a healing. If I don't find anything—meaning the person is clean and clear—there's nothing for me to remove.

A lot of people have the misunderstanding that an in-person healing is stronger or more effective than healing at a distance, which isn't the case. It doesn't matter whether the person I'm working on is sitting across from me in the same room or across town or on the other side of the globe. There is no difference in the strength or quality of a healing. Many people are hesitant to believe that, and if they have demons and Reptilians in them, those entities jump on that thought and try to talk people out of having a session. "Oh, well, he's all the way over there. He can't be effective doing anything from that far away." That's another reason I always let people know they're going to face obstacles and roadblocks if they want to see me or have a session with me. One of those obstacles is the mind chatter from the demons and Reptilians. But once someone makes the conscious decision to change—to have those entities removed—and commits to having a session, that's when the healing actually begins.

Whether the session is going to be by telephone or in person, I start preparing well ahead of time. I may not be consciously working on the person, but energetically the work has already begun. Some people can feel it, and they tell me they were aware of me or the guides working on them. If the entities are being particularly disruptive and bothering the person before we're able to have our session, I ask the Arcturians or Archangel Michael to neutralize them and to provide protection for the person until we can actually remove the entities.

Yes, I could remove them then and there—and sometimes I do—but many people like to experience the removals. And there are some who I feel should experience the removals, especially those who are more skeptical.

For anyone who is doing removals, including me, the preparation is at least as important as the work that takes place in the actual healing session. In fact, it's essential. You simply cannot do the healing if you don't adequately prepare yourself. So I always give myself plenty of time, whether I need fifteen minutes or an hour. I want to be at my best for the benefit of everyone involved.

During

Normally I do the healings in a light channeled state, and they take a little bit of time to complete. This isn't a five-minute process, even though I'm getting faster, more efficient, and more effective all the time.

It's extremely important to work on only one person at a time, and to take your time with each person. If you have several people lined up to work on in the same session, whether in person or at a distance, you're bringing whatever they have into the energetic mix, which confuses things. Don't put any other names on the table; don't go anywhere else until you finish with the person you're focused on. Go slowly and make sure you've removed everything—or at least everything you can remove in that particular session. The guides will let you know if the person has had all he or she can handle at that time.

At the beginning of a session, I bring in the Arcturians first, before any other guides. I ask them to send that shaft of light right down through the person's crown chakra and all the way down so it's grounded. That pierces the veil the Reptilians use to prevent anyone from sensing them. It takes their power away because when the veil or force field is there, you can't penetrate it. Psychically, you can't see through it. Even if you know the Reptilians are there, and you ask the soul's permission to remove them, it's the Reptilians who will respond, and they will always say, "No, you do not have permission."

If there are Reptilians present, I can sense the Arcturians automatically turning that shaft of light into a vortex. The vortex takes the Reptilians up just like a pneumatic tube at the drive-up window of a bank. But the shaft of light—which is a high-vibrational healing and cleansing light—remains in place throughout the session, even after the Reptilians are gone, or even if there were no Reptilians in that person. The shaft of light helps raise the vibration of the person we're working on.

Any demons that are present immediately begin engaging me, so I concentrate on removing them first. The Reptilians usually sacrifice some demons right away, since they can control them. Do be polite when you're communicating with Star Beings and Ascended Masters and remember to say "please" and "thank you," but also bear in mind they can't entirely feel what you're feeling. So when you're engaged in removing these entities and you have multiple demons coming at you, it's appropriate to say *now*: "Now, Michael. Take them *now*." And *whoosh*, it's done. With experience, you begin to develop the certainty that what you ask for in healing and removal will be done. In the beginning, you may be a little unsure. It's part of the learning process. But eventually you will know.

After those demons are gone, the Arcturians will take the Reptilians. It's critical to ask the Arcturians to also remove the eggs. And whenever you cleanse a person, always remember to cleanse not only his or her home, but also the entire property and any vehicles of all entities and of eggs. Check to see if there are any portals where the person lives. If there are portals there, the Arcturians will tell you how many and how long it will take to clear them. The Arcturians will disable the homing device and reconfigure the person's genetic code, which takes three weeks. We don't do it; we simply acknowledge that it's being done, and the Arcturians take care of it.

The Arcturians will let you know if the person has bloodline Reptilians. Initially, I heard the actual word, "bloodline," but now, as soon as the Arcturians begin removing Reptilians, I can tell if they're in the bloodline. The Arcturians have trained me to be able to sense it. It's a different kind of energy. And it's very strong. Removing Reptilians from the bloodline is a much more in-depth and powerful process than just removing them from the DNA, and it takes longer. The first time I did it, it took me over an hour of intense energy and concentration. Now I don't find it as difficult or time consuming.

When someone has Reptilians in them, you can expect to have maybe two or three sessions, but the first session is usually the most intense. A lot of the work I've done on people has taken place in stages, like peeling an onion. Don't try to make it a sprint to the finish line. It's possible for it to all happen in a rush, with everything going at once, but it rarely does happen that way. The entities leave in waves, and every so often, one of those waves is a big one. After the Reptilians are gone, Jesus will go in. Then there may be another round or more of demons to remove. Attachments often leave at the same time as the demons, but sometimes they go later.

Discarnates tend to be the last of the entities to leave. Since discarnates and attachments don't have the same intense energy as the demons and Reptilians, their presence can be easy to miss. So continue looking and scanning to see if there's anything else. When I sense something else is still there, but I'm not sure what it is, I'll ask Archangel Michael if he can take it to the Light. If it's an attachment, he'll take it. If it doesn't go, then I know it's most likely a discarnate. The angels and archangels and other guides don't treat discarnates—human souls—the same way they treat demons or Reptilians. They have more respect and compassion for them; they know who they are so they treat them gently.

Discarnates don't normally come individually to hurt or harm someone, but they are often controlled by demons or Reptilians. It isn't until after the demons and Reptilians are gone that I can sense them. All you have to say to the discarnates is, "Just look up." Maybe they did look up at one time, when they died, or maybe they already tried crossing over, but they were blocked or afraid and didn't want to go. But now Jesus has gone into the person, the shaft or vortex of light is there, and the angelic realm is up above at the opening. The heavens are lit up, and now the discarnates can see the Light. Once they see the Light, they don't take much convincing to leave. *Whoosh!* I can feel it when they go. Sometimes there's only one. Sometimes there are several. I always feel a lot better after they've gone to the Light. About two-thirds of the time, I get a major back-flash of unconditional love and appreciation from the soul that just left.

After all the entities are gone, Archangel Raphael starts looking for other things. You may start seeing cords—which can be attached to other people, to places or things, or even to past lives—being cut.

Don't be afraid to let people know what you're doing and what's happening during the session. I always tell them. If they think I'm nuts, that's OK. But I have never yet had a negative reaction from someone after I've told them. I think intuitively they know, and they appreciate my being forthright and truthful with them.

Remind people that the healing process takes three to six weeks and that they should take extra-good care of themselves during that time.

It's like having major surgery without having been sliced open. They will need to be ready for anything, physically, emotionally, mentally, and spiritually, since they'll be going on a roller coaster ride for at least three weeks. In fact, I tell people to mark both the three-week and the six-week points on their calendars as reminders.

After the first healing session, people sometimes continue hearing mind chatter from the entities and may think whatever was removed has returned. That's never the case. Once something goes to the Light, it cannot return. But it's always possible you won't remove everything in the course of the first healing session. Some people have so many current or past-life issues to deal with that it's almost impossible to remove everything in one session. That's why I suggest up to three sessions over the course of that six-week period. The first session can be exceptionally intense, so I always suggest another session about three weeks later, when the DNA has been reconfigured, and maybe another one at the six-week point.

How intense the recovery process will be and how long it will take to get through depends on a number of variables. What type and how many entities were removed? How long did the person have them? Did the person have Reptilians, and if so, were they bloodline Reptilians? Is the person already doing his or her work and trying to become enlightened? The more entities and attachments a person has had removed, the more dramatic the effects of the healing will be. If someone only has discarnates, they might not experience much during the recovery period. But if someone has had entities—especially multiple entities—for decades, he or she can expect to have a longer and more intense recovery.

You can find more information about the recovery process following a Divine Healing session, as well as about demons, discarnates, attachments, and cords, in Chapter 2.

After

When you're finished with the removals, there's one more extremely important thing to do before closing the session. Ask for a cleansing for whoever is present or whoever has been energetically involved to make sure no residue from any of these entities has sloughed off onto anyone, including you. Cleanse all of those people, cleanse yourself, and cleanse the space you're working in with lots of white light.

When the session is over, close the channel and let it go. Drop it. Move on with your own life. It's important not to carry all of this around with you. When I first started doing this, I would leave the channel open—which is like leaving your crown chakra wide open—and I would continually be bombarded with more information about the person. I found that I kept thinking and thinking about it to the point where it was affecting the rest of my life. I learned the hard way that you have to shut it down. And you have to do that intentionally. So now, when I'm done, I'm done.

Because I'm in a light channeled state during a session, I may forget as much as 95% of what happens. I always tell people that ahead of time so they're not offended afterward when I don't remember something. That's one of the reasons I record these sessions.

All of this work requires intense focus and concentration, and that can take a lot of your energy. The process may sound easy—and in some ways, it is—but you will be affected energetically. Whether you're affected positively or negatively will depend on how you're able to handle all these different energies. When you first start doing this, expect to feel tired and drained afterward, so schedule your healing sessions with that in mind. It's imperative that you take care of yourself, that you're in good physical and mental health, and that you keep your vibration up. Remember that we're dealing with very low, negative, dense energies and low vibrational frequencies from the demons, discarnates, and Reptilians. On the other end of the spectrum, Jesus and the Arcturians and the angelic realm all have much higher vibrational frequencies. They all have to lower their frequencies a little to come down to our level, and we have to raise ours higher so we can meet in between in order to do the work.

I used to feel drained afterward, too, but I don't anymore. I always raise my vibration before a session, as I've said, but even though I may get bombarded during a healing, by the time we're done, I feel energized and light, and my vibration is even higher. I feel good after these sessions. That's the beautiful side benefit of working with the Arcturians and the angelic realm and Jesus. But remember that I've been doing these removals for a while.

Right after you finish a session you might find yourself on a natural high. Your vibration is high so you may think you're impervious to anything. But you need to be cautious. Before you attempt to do another healing session, stop, slow down, get centered and balanced, go in, meditate, and make sure your own vibration is raised and you're connected. Then you'll be ready for more.

Why We Do This Work

There is nothing easy about any of this. The work is not for the faint of heart. But it needs to be done, so I think it's worth the risk. When people who have demons and/or Reptilians come in for a session, I can sometimes see it in their eyes—especially if they have demons. It's fear. They're looking out at me through all that mental chatter going on inside them. But after we remove everything, their eyes are clear and they're lighter. They look happier, relaxed, more at peace. You can see the difference in their faces. A one-hour session can make that much difference.

Every time one of these Reptilians, demons, or discarnates goes to the Light, the vibration of that person improves, the vibration of everyone that person comes in contact with improves, the vibration of the planet improves, and we get closer to the fifth dimension. That's why we're doing all of this: to help heal every individual and planet Earth—*one soul or millions at a time.*

Chapter 15
Expanding The Boundaries

Healing the Dead

S
ince working on Julia's deceased husband, Paul, who I described in Chapter 10, I've worked on quite a few other deceased individuals. I find it fascinating the work can be done on this level. Recently, I had a session with a very sensitive and aware woman whose husband had died two or three years ago. She had been doing her own work, and her husband had been doing his work, too, while he was alive. She'd assumed he had been clear when he died and that he had crossed over.

I've learned that when I work on someone, I also need to work on that person's immediate family members and anyone they mention who has passed away. In this case, the woman told me she hadn't been able to sense her deceased husband much anymore. "It's like he's gone off and moved somewhere else." I asked her if she was sure he'd gone to the Light. She didn't know; she wasn't able to feel him. People often assume their relatives or loved ones who have died have crossed over. But when I ask them directly if they're sure, it turns out that most of the time they're not. They want to believe it, of course; they don't want to consider the other option.

I couldn't sense this woman's husband, either. All I saw was darkness. I couldn't see his light. Then as soon as we started focusing on him, I got that pinch in the neck, and I started feeling nauseous. Archangel Michael immediately began removing demons, and then the Arcturians removed the Reptilians. The Arcturians can do their work on these souls easier and faster than they can on the living because they don't have to deal with a physical body. The DNA is reconfigured instantly instead of requiring a three-week process. The imprint is removed right then and there.

Once the demons and Reptilians were removed, I was able to sense her husband. At that point, there was a little conversation back and forth between the two of them. Then, I told him, "OK, it's time for you to go to the Light now." The angels don't always do this, but in this instance, they helped him go to the Light. The energy and appreciation I felt from him was tremendous. I saw his light then. I mean, he just lit up. And I got that back-flash of unconditional love I often get when discarnates go to the Light.

Healers, mediums, or psychics who don't know they need to check for Reptilians can be very easily misled into thinking the deceased person has crossed over. Not only can the demons and Reptilians block people from going to the Light after they die, that veil the Reptilians put up can block *our* perception of what is actually going on. That's why I wasn't picking up on him or feeling him at first.

He didn't have the bloodline, but he had died with Reptilians and demons and had not been able to cross over. He was stuck in limbo. Without being healed, he would have remained there, unable to come back in another incarnation. Some souls who have the Reptilian or demon imprint on them are able to cross over, but they bring that imprint—and the entities—back with them in their next incarnations.

Prior to about six months ago, I wasn't doing this type of work as often because I didn't know you could heal the dead. I thought that once a person was dead, that was it. He or she was gone, and what we did on earth couldn't affect them. I didn't know we could cross that boundary to heal them, but now I'm doing it more and more frequently. It's part of the evolution of this healing work.

Creating Large-Scale Vortexes

Another aspect of the evolution or expansion of the work involves creating large-scale vortexes, sometimes several miles in diameter, which clear out all the entities from a particular area although right now they don't remove the entities that are possessing the people inside that area.

The first time I was involved in creating a large-scale vortex was during my weekend camping trip in the mountains in the summer of 2009, which I described in the Introduction. I had just completed the series of channeling classes and had been working on individuals to remove demons, discarnates, and attachments and send them to the Light. Much of that work was still new to me and, as I've said, I was playing catch up in an effort to understand what was going on. I had no idea how many more surprises were still in store for me. I hadn't yet encountered the Arcturians and discovered I was connected with them. Nor did I know anything about the Reptilians. It took the series of sessions with Carl in the fall of that year for all of those pieces to begin coming together.

Once I came in contact with the Arcturians and accepted their download, I began to work with them on a regular basis whenever I was doing removals and healings. In the spring of the year after the sessions with Carl, I started doing a lot of large-scale vortex work, especially around the Southwest United States. That first vortex took me by surprise, but once I started doing them more often, I knew exactly what was going on. It felt like a natural progression.

How It Works

One way or another, the Arcturians will manage to get my attention as to where they want a vortex created. They may use a person or a place, but whatever it is, I always understand what they mean. They guide, inspire, or lead me to go to a particular location. I don't actually need to be physically present in that location in order to get the vortex going, but I prefer to be there if possible. I like to see it and experience it. It's interesting to watch how the birds or animals within the vortexes react. Some of them make all kinds of racket, like the ravens who start cawing incessantly and the bull in that meadow that wouldn't stop bellowing. The energy feels really charged.

If I'm going to go out someplace and do this in person, I start with protection beforehand. Once I get there, I call in the Arcturians, and I begin creating the vortex. I've gotten into the habit of twirling my pointer finger upward—which I'm sure isn't necessary—but I like to participate in the process. Twirling my finger is my way of sort of directing the orchestra. Once the vortex gets going, Jesus stands in the middle, above it. He doesn't come down in these types of situations.

Then the energy starts coursing through me, and I'll get confirmation as to whatever is there: a pinch on the neck if there are Reptilians; nausea if there are demons. I'll bring in warrior and protection angels just for this particular vortex. There are a lot of different kinds of angels, but since this is spiritual warfare, I expressly ask for warrior and protection angels. Then I ask Archangel Michael to start taking the demons up to the Light. I can't see them, but I sense them. Usually they're going up right and left. First, we clear all of the demons that are floating around waiting to attack someone.

Sometimes other guides will come in. Often Archangel Gabriel comes in or maybe Mother Mary—not only in these situations, but in individual work, as well. When I'm doing a healing session for someone, often that person's own guides come through to participate in the process.

Once Archangel Michael has taken the demons to the Light, we keep the vortex going, and I ask the Arcturians to start taking all the Reptilians within this vortex up to the Light. It's the same sequence I use in individual work. But in these large-scale vortexes, we're only removing the Reptilians that are outside people. If there are portals underground, the Arcturians let me know how many, and they send a shaft of light down into each one as far as it needs to go. Then they begin neutralizing the Reptilians. The shaft of light also works the same in one of these vortexes as it does for an individual. It pierces the veil to expose the Reptilians, and it stuns them so they can't escape.

Other Reptilians may try to come in for a rescue, but once they're in the vortex, they won't be able to get out. It's like birds flying into a window. *Thunk!* They're temporarily knocked unconscious. In my mind's eye I see the Reptilians as dark little Gumbies floating up inside the vortex. The Arcturians tell me how long it's going to take to clean out the portals. Sometimes it's just a day, other times it's a few days or even as long as two weeks. It depends on how many portals there are and how deep into the earth they go. Some of these vortexes can be as large as 15 to 30 miles in diameter. So far, I've only been involved in one that was larger than that.

Once I stop feeling that pinch in the neck, I know the Reptilians are no longer harassing me, so I can let them go. Just as the Arcturians do in an individual session, they then remove all the eggs that are within the vortex.

A Wasp' Nest of Demons

There may be another wave of demons for Archangel Michael to remove. I've had demons come at me like a swarm of wasps in some situations. I was traveling out of state a couple of years ago, before I had even started doing this large-scale vortex work, and stopped at an historical site. It was at the end of a winding road about half a mile off the highway and had signs everywhere marking spots where battles had taken place during different wars. The entire area was full of negative energy, although at the time I didn't know why. I was on vacation and just looking for a souvenir for my brother, and I went inside a building I really didn't feel comfortable entering. I stuck my head into a back room where eight or ten people were sitting around a circle listening to a man who was singing country western songs. Not only were every one of those people possessed, but the entire area was being used as a sort of demonic pick-up spot. People came there to drink and listen to summer concerts and were unknowingly opening themselves up to possession.

I slowly walked back to the front of the building, stood aside, and called in my guides. Archangel Michael began removing the demons that were roaming around there—as well as the demons inside those eight or ten people. Fortunately, when I'm removing demons on this kind of scale, I don't experience the gagging reflex I have when I'm removing them from an individual. That would be too much, too intense. I wouldn't be able to do the work if I had to go through that.

Suddenly, I felt an overwhelming urge to leave the place. Just get out. I still didn't know why. But I got into my car, and as I was heading out the winding dirt road back toward the highway, another car pulled in front of me. I had a moment of panic because I thought the car was going to slow me down, and I really wanted to get away from that place. But all of a sudden the car disappeared. Maybe it pulled over somewhere. I don't know what happened to it. As soon as it was gone, I took off.

When I got onto the highway, I felt a swarm of demons coming at me just like wasps. The hair on the back of my neck stood up, and as I was driving down the highway, I sensed the battle going on behind me between Archangel Michael and the warrior and protection angels and that swarm of demons. These demons were not from the site but had come from the surrounding area to extract revenge. They were furious at having their activity at the site disrupted. I haven't felt or experienced anything that chilling before or since, and I'm very grateful for the protection of the angels. Of course, they were aware I did not go to that place to get a physical gift for my brother, but to be part of a healing gift for the whole area.

That's why I say this is spiritual warfare and you can't take it lightly. You've got to make sure you're well protected and you're ready. I wasn't totally prepared to encounter what I did at that historical site. But that was an unusual situation. Now, I know what I'm going to be doing or getting into ahead of time. And if I find myself in a situation like this one, I call on the Arcturians and get a vortex going. I hadn't gone to that particular place in order to create one—or even to do any removals—so what happened caught me off-guard. As a result, I had to react quickly. Thank God, my vibrational frequency was high.

The Arcturians Finish the Job

The next thing that happens is the discarnates go. Remember, the vortex opens up to the heavens. Jesus is already standing up there in the middle, and the angels are swirling around the outside of it. It isn't uncommon for me to call in a million or more angels for one of these large-scale vortexes. So I say to the discarnates, "All right, everybody, just look up. Just look up." When they look up, they can see the Light; they can see Jesus and the angels. I can feel them go, just like that. Often, discarnates have demons or Reptilians attached to them, so we have to make sure all the demons and Reptilians are gone. If any of them are still there, they won't let the discarnates go. That's why we do the removals in this particular sequence. *You have to neutralize the Reptilians because they can control the demons. And you have to neutralize and remove the demons, because they can control the discarnates.*

Once all the entities have been removed, there's nothing else for me to do. The Arcturians, whose vortex it really is, will stay with it until they're finished clearing out the portals, and then they'll shut them down permanently. I don't know how many Arcturian space ships are present working any particular vortex. They bring in as many as they need to do the job.

Most people who are sensitive to these kinds of energies tell me afterward that the area feels lighter, peaceful, and more comfortable. The energy isn't as heavy or dense.

Vortexes Near and Far

These vortexes can be created anywhere. The Arcturians have guided me to a lot of different places around the Southwest to do them. I've traveled to a number of Native American locations and a lot of the historic sites and national monuments around here. At one remote area of ruins I had first visited nearly 20 years ago, I was clearly warned by some type of dark energy to get out. I wasn't welcome there. So I left and stayed away from it until about a year and a half ago when a friend wanted to visit the site. It wasn't a pleasant experience. The energy was still very dense and negative. It felt oppressive and suffocating. I've since cleared it of the demons that were there, and when I went back later, they were gone, and the place felt much better. But a lot of people visit places like that, so who knows how many people were infected by those demons over the period of time when they were there.

At another similar location, I encountered quite a few discarnates who had been hanging around for maybe hundreds or even thousands of years guarding the place. After we got the vortex going, all but one of them left. He was the final warrior protector for that site, and he did not want to go even when we told him to look up. Finally, the angels told him his time here was done. It was time for him to leave so he could come back and help in another capacity. He understood that and agreed to go. When he left, some angels escorted him up to the Light.

When I first started doing these vortexes, I took pictures at each of the locations. In one place, I photographed an area inside some cliff dwellings where people had once lived, both before starting the vortex and after the removals. In the pictures taken after the removals, there are small orbs of light that aren't in the first set of pictures. I don't have a ready explanation for them. All I can say is that the energy afterward felt very good.

A Large Hospital

Sometimes, as I mentioned, the Arcturians might lead me to create one of these vortexes in the course of my contact with a person I'm working with. In one such instance, I met with a couple in order to do some work on their son. Although I didn't think the husband and wife needed any work, I checked them just to be sure everyone was clean and clear before I started on their son. As soon as I went in to check the wife, *whoosh*, just like that the Arcturians led me to the large hospital where she worked. That place was loaded. There were five portals under the hospital, and the Arcturians worked on it for five days before it was completely cleared out.

After getting that vortex going through the hospital and down into the ground over the entire property, I started working on the couple's son, who lives in another state. We cleared both him and his wife, and then the Arcturians immediately guided me to expand the vortex to 15 miles in diameter to cover the entire small town where the couple lived. When I spoke to the parents after they visited their son, they told me he was going through the emotional roller coaster ride people often experience after entities have been removed. But they said the whole town felt so much lighter and more energetic. It wasn't as dense and dark as it had felt to them during their previous visits.

Two Nuclear Facilities

One of the most interesting vortexes I was involved in was at Los Alamos National Laboratory, which was founded during World War II to develop atomic and nuclear weapons. An acquaintance of mine who is psychic took a trip through that area and told me later about some of the strange experiences she had. It was already on my list, so a couple of weeks after talking to her, I went in and we got a vortex going.

Reptilians weren't the only negative energies that needed to be removed, so it wasn't just the Arcturians who came through on that one. The Andromedans were there, as was the whole Galactic Federation, which I bring in whenever things don't feel right to me or when there's something the Arcturians don't appear to have dominion over. It was a major operation. They kept that vortex going for two weeks, which is the longest one I'm aware of.

I'm a catalyst for getting the vortex started, but once it gets going, I'm out of the picture. The Arcturians finish their work without me. I did go in periodically during those two weeks on this one just to take a look and see what was happening. I do that quite often when the Arcturians keep a vortex going for a while. So I scanned every few days, and it looked to me like the original portal wasn't very deep, but the vortex kept going down, down, down through all these different levels of subterranean chambers clearing them one at a time. It was just like taking an elevator ride down to the next group of rooms, then the next group of rooms, and then the next group of rooms. These tunnels don't just dead end; they lead into and connect with larger underground caverns or bases or with other tunnels. I have no idea how many of those chambers there were, but it seemed to take one or two days to clear out each one.

I've also worked with the Arcturians to clear Sandia National Laboratories, which is another facility dedicated to nuclear weapons. I actually saw Reptilians standing guard over the stockpiled nuclear weapons. It was one of the more chilling images I've ever seen.

Removing all these entities raises the vibrational frequency of places like Los Alamos or Sandia. But these locations are natural targets for Reptilians and demons, since they want the kind of fear and anger and aggression those facilities represent. They latch right onto it.

Mt. Shasta

In Chapter 6, I described the first time I was on the ship Athena and visited the planet Arcturus with two women who were also connected with the Arcturians. After we returned from our trip to Arcturus, the topic of Mt. Shasta came up. When I told them I felt I had work to do over there, they suggested we check it out. I wasn't aware I could do something like that. I had done a little remote viewing before, but this was the first time I did it intentionally or directly.

When I got to Mt. Shasta and looked down over it from above, I saw what looked like a black mass of snakes, a den of Reptilians, in one section of the mountain. It was disgusting. So I just broke it off and came back. That was all I needed to see to confirm what I already intuitively knew: Mt. Shasta needed to be cleansed of the Reptilians. At that time it obviously wasn't 100% pure.

I really wanted to go to Mt. Shasta in person to do the work, but I haven't had the opportunity to go there yet. So several months later, I went back remotely and cleared it of Reptilians.

Mexico City

In my travels, I'll sometimes pass through or by an area, like Gettysburg National Cemetery, for example, assuming it needs to be cleared. But when I go in to check, I won't sense very much. There isn't much of anything there. When I ask what's going on, I've been told other people have been releasing demons and discarnates from the area for years.

On the other hand, some places you might expect need to be cleared, like Los Alamos National Laboratory and Sandia National Laboratory, really *do* need clearing. One of the largest vortexes I've ever participated in creating was over Mexico City. In fact, that's the vortex depicted on the cover of this book. I've never been to Mexico City, but the Arcturians led me to do the work at a distance, from my home, and we created a vortex 30 miles in diameter. Something particularly interesting happened with this one. I was sitting with my eyes closed and sensed the vortex was over the western or northwestern part of the city. I have no idea what the terrain is like over there, but I felt the vortex kind of slide up along one side, as if it were going up some mountains. Afterward, I checked an online map, and sure enough, there are mountains in that region.

There were so many portals under Mexico City that the Arcturians worked that vortex for several days. Imagine how many Reptilians, demons, and discarnates left that place during that time. When the discarnates were going up to the Light, they appeared to me as a black mass. It was huge. When I did the very first vortex on that camping trip and asked how many had gone to the Light, the answer I got was "2,000." When I asked this time, the answer was "2,000,000!" That's two million souls cleared and taken to the Light all at once.

Once a vortex is finished, Reptilians, demons, and discarnates are free to return to that area—not the ones who were removed and went to the Light, but others. A couple of months after that 30-mile vortex was finished, the Arcturians had me create another one, and this time they expanded it to 60 miles in diameter, which is the largest vortex I've been involved in creating so far. I'm not entirely sure why they had me go back to expand it. Maybe it's a matter of resources; maybe the Arcturians can only take so many Reptilians at a time. But this kind of thing may need to be done on a regular basis in order to keep an area clear, so I'll go back and do it again at some point if I'm led or inspired to do it.

Raising the Vibration of the Planet

Even if we do have to go back and clear it again, look at all the negativity that left that one location. Removing all those Reptilians and demons and discarnates from an area that size improves the vibration of the area tremendously. I wasn't there in Mexico City, and I didn't have anyone on the ground to check in with, but I know it makes the energy lighter and clearer. It has to affect the entire city and all the people in it. But not only does it affect that specific area and those particular people, it also affects the entire planet.

However, so far we haven't been able to clear or remove the entities that are inside the people who are in these large-scale vortexes. We create vortexes to clear individuals, and then we create them for these large-scale clearings or removals. But even though it's the same healing process in both situations, with the larger vortexes, we haven't been able to get to the entities inside the people.

Although, it didn't involve creating a vortex, the situation at that historical site in Texas was an exception in that Archangel Michael removed demons from inside several individuals at the same time. And while I was finishing this book, I was reminded of another situation that occurred around the same period of time that I had forgotten about.

On two occasions during Christmas Eve services at a local mega-church, I also experienced Michael removing entities from inside a number of people at the same time. Because it was Christmas Eve, the church was packed both with adults and with children who were attending Sunday school classes. I don't know the exact number of children who were present at each of the services I attended, but they numbered in the hundreds—maybe as many as 1,500. I was led to ask my guides to clear all of the children, and in one instance, I received a message that something like 300 demons were released from those children. Now children are more resilient than a lot of older adults, and they haven't had entities inside them for decades, so maybe they're easier to clear in a group. And these were demons, not Reptilians, that were removed, both from the children and from those people in Texas. So I'm not sure what the explanation is. Maybe the ability is already present, and I need to develop it and exercise it.

I hadn't gone to that church with the intention of clearing anyone— just as I hadn't had that intention when I was on vacation in Texas— so of course I didn't have my tape recorder in either situation and don't have any documentation of them like I have of all the one-on-one or group sessions. But you can't always document every instance of clearing someone. I do it so often now, frequently on the spur of the moment when I'm out and about, that it's become almost commonplace.

I think we somehow have to get to the point where we can routinely remove all the entities inside people, including Reptilians, during the course of these large-scale vortexes. I envision it happening. I know the Arcturians can do it. The limitation right now is probably me.

It would be wonderful to line up a thousand people—or even ten thousand—in an auditorium and do a mass removal. After an hour session, we could tell them, "All right, everyone here, whatever you had is gone." Is that possible? I think it is. Even though I'm not there yet, intuitively I believe it's going to happen. I think that's the natural progression—that's where all this work is leading. Right now, we can heal millions of discarnates—deceased souls—all at once. We should also be able to heal millions of living souls all at once.

Chapter 16
Waking Up To The Truth

S omeone recently asked me how the experiences I've described in this book have affected me or how they've changed my life. I was at a loss as to how to answer that question, not because they haven't affected me, but because of the degree to which they have. It's hard to explain, but I'm not the same. My life has been turned upside down and inside out, in a positive way, and has gone in directions I couldn't possibly have dreamt it would. Me—a redneck farm boy from Iowa—35 years as a private investigator—and now I'm channeling? Checking in with Star Beings and extraterrestrials? Removing demons and alien Reptilians?

I had no intention of getting into any of this when I went to that first channeling class. Given where I had come from, how could I have even imagined it? All I wanted to do was learn how to better connect with Spirit and with my guides. Then after I learned how to connect with them, I discovered they had something for me to do. That's one thing you can take from my experience: find out who your guides are and learn how to connect with them. You may find they have something for you to do, too.

You have to be open to it. Although I was very skeptical at first, I went into this with an open mind, and I've tried to keep an open mind. I don't know everything. What's in this book is what I'm aware of today, but it's an evolving picture, like a scroll that's being unrolled before me one day at a time. I have no idea what I'll find out tomorrow, but I'm excited about it.

When I asked the Arcturians what else they wanted me to communicate to you at this time, one of the things they said was:

Wake up; sleep no longer. Become aware of the truth that surrounds you at every turn.

That's it. That's the key. For me, this has been a process of waking up from a deep sleep.

The Arcturians also had this to say:

Namaste and many blessings, our brothers and sisters of the light.

Rejoice in your new knowledge and go forth with your heart and mind as one. Look inward, listen to your heart in silence, and you will know the truth that will set you free. Balance your life with the best of both the masculine and the feminine. Become one with the All That Is and Ever Was and Ever Will Be.

The souls of the people of Mother Earth have suffered enough over the ages, and now is the time to make the Age of Aquarius a new and glorious era.

If you decide to undertake this life-changing process, you will face challenges, but I believe the benefits for you and for this planet are worth the risks. The greater danger lies in remaining ignorant and in denial. Of course, you need to be prepared, but you don't need to be afraid. The Reptilians want you to be afraid—they feed off of your fear. Know that the Arcturians, who are loving and much more powerful than the Reptilians, will protect you and your loved ones if you call upon them.

Now that you are aware of the Reptilians, please don't dwell on them or focus on the darkness. Remember that thoughts are like magnets. What you give your attention to attracts more of the same, so be positive. Focus on love and light. Focus on the Arcturians. Keep your auric shield strong. Raise your vibrational frequency a little bit more each day until keeping your vibration high becomes a way of life.

Do not let this book sit on a shelf in obscurity. If you are not led or inspired to take up the call, pass it along to someone you know and love who needs help or who could use this information to benefit mankind.

Whether we realize it or not, we are all one; so be joyful and grateful, and above all, love one another. Let's take back our lives and become one again with each other and with all things of the Light.

About the Author

Wayne Brewer, author of *Are You Possessed? Now Is the Time for Divine Intervention*, is a prominent private investigator with over 35 years of experience uncovering hidden truths. He has put his P.I. skills to use in the spiritual realm and, with the help of his multidimensional guides, has discovered an ability and developed a technique for effectively removing *entities*—discarnate spirits, demons, and alien Reptilians—and sending them to the Light. He uses these gifts and techniques in his International Spirit Releasement practice. Through his experience performing in-person and long-distance clearings, he has assisted thousands of people on their journeys to personal empowerment.

Wayne is available to work with you individually or in group workshops and can help you learn how to connect with the Arcturians and conduct healings. He is also available for speaking engagements, workshops, and radio and TV interviews. He has worked with individuals all over the world and can travel to your city or country.

Contact Wayne for your own personal healing session, to assist a loved one, or to conduct a large-scale healing vortex for your community. Keep abreast of the latest news and events by visiting his website and signing up for his free periodic newsletter.

www.WayneBrewer.net

Made in the USA
Las Vegas, NV
02 April 2021

20659078R00125